Platform Positioning
Complete Self-Assessment Guide

Table of Contents

About The Art of Service

The Art of Service, Business Process Architects since 2000, is dedicated to helping stakeholders achieve excellence.

Defining, designing, creating, and implementing a process to solve a stakeholders challenge or meet an objective is the most valuable role... In EVERY group, company, organization and department.

Unless you're talking a one-time, single-use project, there should be a process. Whether that process is managed and implemented by humans, AI, or a combination of the two, it needs to be designed by someone with a complex enough perspective to ask the right questions.

Someone capable of asking the right questions and step back and say, 'What are we really trying to accomplish here? And is there a different way to look at it?'

With The Art of Service's Standard Requirements Self-Assessments, we empower people who can do just that — whether their title is marketer, entrepreneur, manager, salesperson, consultant, Business Process Manager, executive assistant, IT Manager, CIO etc... —they are the people who rule the future. They are people who watch the process as it happens, and ask the right questions to make the process work better.

Contact us when you need any support with this Self-Assessment and any help with templates, blue-prints and examples of standard documents you might need:

http://theartofservice.com
service@theartofservice.com

Included Resources - how to access

Included with your purchase of the book is the Platform

Positioning Self-Assessment Spreadsheet Dashboard which contains all questions and Self-Assessment areas and auto-generates insights, graphs, and project RACI planning - all with examples to get you started right away.

How? Simply send an email to
access@theartofservice.com
with this books' title in the subject to get the Platform Positioning Self Assessment Tool right away.

You will receive the following contents with New and Updated specific criteria:

- The latest quick edition of the book in PDF

- The latest complete edition of the book in PDF, which criteria correspond to the criteria in...

- The Self-Assessment Excel Dashboard, and...

- Example pre-filled Self-Assessment Excel Dashboard to get familiar with results generation

- In-depth specific Checklists covering the topic

- Project management checklists and templates to assist with implementation

Purpose of this Self-Assessment

This Self-Assessment has been developed to improve understanding of the requirements and elements of Platform Positioning, based on best practices and standards in business process architecture, design and quality management.

It is designed to allow for a rapid Self-Assessment to determine how closely existing management practices and procedures correspond to the elements of the Self-Assessment.

The criteria of requirements and elements of Platform Positioning have been rephrased in the format of a Self-Assessment questionnaire, with a seven-criterion scoring system, as explained in this document.

In this format, even with limited background knowledge of Platform Positioning, a manager can quickly review existing operations to determine how they measure up to the standards. This in turn can serve as the starting point of a 'gap analysis' to identify management tools or system elements that might usefully be implemented in the organization to help improve overall performance.

How to use the Self-Assessment

On the following pages are a series of questions to identify to what extent your Platform Positioning initiative is complete in comparison to the requirements set in standards.

To facilitate answering the questions, there is a space in front of each question to enter a score on a scale of '1' to '5'.

1 Strongly Disagree

2 Disagree

3 Neutral

4 Agree

5 Strongly Agree

Read the question and rate it with the following in front of mind:

'In my belief,
the answer to this question is clearly defined'.

There are two ways in which you can choose to interpret this statement;
1. how aware are you that the answer to the question is clearly defined
2. for more in-depth analysis you can choose to gather evidence and confirm the answer to the question. This obviously will take more time, most Self-Assessment users opt for the first way to interpret the question and dig deeper later on based on the outcome of the overall Self-Assessment.

A score of '1' would mean that the answer is not clear at all, where a '5' would mean the answer is crystal clear and defined. Leave emtpy when the question is not applicable or you don't want to answer it, you can skip it without affecting your score. Write your score in the space provided.

After you have responded to all the appropriate statements in each section, compute your average score for that section, using the formula provided, and round to the nearest tenth. Then transfer to the corresponding spoke in the Platform Positioning Scorecard on the second next page of the Self-Assessment.

Your completed Platform Positioning Scorecard will give you a clear presentation of which Platform Positioning areas need attention.

Platform Positioning
Scorecard Example

Example of how the finalized Scorecard can look like:

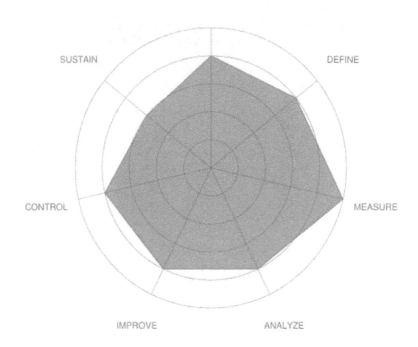

Platform Positioning Scorecard

Your Scores:

BEGINNING OF THE SELF-ASSESSMENT:

CRITERION #1: RECOGNIZE

INTENT: Be aware of the need for change. Recognize that there is an unfavorable variation, problem or symptom.

In my belief, the answer to this question is clearly defined:

5 Strongly Agree

4 Agree

3 Neutral

2 Disagree

1 Strongly Disagree

1. Is it clear when you think of the day ahead of you what activities and tasks you need to complete?
<--- Score

2. What is the extent or complexity of the Platform Positioning problem?
<--- Score

3. How are the Platform Positioning's objectives aligned to the group's overall stakeholder strategy?
<--- Score

4. Are problem definition and motivation clearly presented?
<--- Score

5. What does Platform Positioning success mean to the stakeholders?
<--- Score

6. Which issues are too important to ignore?
<--- Score

7. To what extent would your organization benefit from being recognized as a award recipient?
<--- Score

8. How do you take a forward-looking perspective in identifying Platform Positioning research related to market response and models?
<--- Score

9. What are the Platform Positioning resources needed?
<--- Score

10. What are the stakeholder objectives to be achieved with Platform Positioning?
<--- Score

11. Who else hopes to benefit from it?
<--- Score

12. What should be considered when identifying

available resources, constraints, and deadlines?
<--- Score

13. How do you recognize an objection?
<--- Score

14. Are you dealing with any of the same issues today as yesterday? What can you do about this?
<--- Score

15. What are the clients issues and concerns?
<--- Score

16. Do you have/need 24-hour access to key personnel?
<--- Score

17. What is the Platform Positioning problem definition? What do you need to resolve?
<--- Score

18. What needs to be done?
<--- Score

19. Do you recognize Platform Positioning achievements?
<--- Score

20. Have you identified your Platform Positioning key performance indicators?
<--- Score

21. How does it fit into your organizational needs and tasks?
<--- Score

22. Will a response program recognize when a crisis occurs and provide some level of response?
<--- Score

23. Which information does the Platform Positioning business case need to include?
<--- Score

24. Who needs budgets?
<--- Score

25. How are you going to measure success?
<--- Score

26. Are there any revenue recognition issues?
<--- Score

27. Would you recognize a threat from the inside?
<--- Score

28. Which needs are not included or involved?
<--- Score

29. What Platform Positioning events should you attend?
<--- Score

30. Who should resolve the Platform Positioning issues?
<--- Score

31. What Platform Positioning coordination do you need?
<--- Score

32. Why is this needed?

<--- Score

33. Consider your own Platform Positioning project, what types of organizational problems do you think might be causing or affecting your problem, based on the work done so far?
<--- Score

34. What tools and technologies are needed for a custom Platform Positioning project?
<--- Score

35. What else needs to be measured?
<--- Score

36. What are the minority interests and what amount of minority interests can be recognized?
<--- Score

37. How many trainings, in total, are needed?
<--- Score

38. How do you assess your Platform Positioning workforce capability and capacity needs, including skills, competencies, and staffing levels?
<--- Score

39. How are training requirements identified?
<--- Score

40. How can auditing be a preventative security measure?
<--- Score

41. How do you recognize an Platform Positioning objection?

<--- Score

42. Why the need?
<--- Score

43. Looking at each person individually – does every one have the qualities which are needed to work in this group?
<--- Score

44. What are the timeframes required to resolve each of the issues/problems?
<--- Score

45. What situation(s) led to this Platform Positioning Self Assessment?
<--- Score

46. For your Platform Positioning project, identify and describe the business environment, is there more than one layer to the business environment?
<--- Score

47. Do you need to avoid or amend any Platform Positioning activities?
<--- Score

48. Does your organization need more Platform Positioning education?
<--- Score

49. Are employees recognized or rewarded for performance that demonstrates the highest levels of integrity?
<--- Score

50. What is the problem and/or vulnerability?
<--- Score

51. Does Platform Positioning create potential expectations in other areas that need to be recognized and considered?
<--- Score

52. Whom do you really need or want to serve?
<--- Score

53. Are there any specific expectations or concerns about the Platform Positioning team, Platform Positioning itself?
<--- Score

54. Will Platform Positioning deliverables need to be tested and, if so, by whom?
<--- Score

55. Who needs to know?
<--- Score

56. What creative shifts do you need to take?
<--- Score

57. What is the recognized need?
<--- Score

58. What do you need to start doing?
<--- Score

59. When a Platform Positioning manager recognizes a problem, what options are available?
<--- Score

60. What prevents you from making the changes you know will make you a more effective Platform Positioning leader?

<--- Score

61. Who needs what information?

<--- Score

62. What would happen if Platform Positioning weren't done?

<--- Score

63. How much are sponsors, customers, partners, stakeholders involved in Platform Positioning? In other words, what are the risks, if Platform Positioning does not deliver successfully?

<--- Score

64. Who defines the rules in relation to any given issue?

<--- Score

65. What training and capacity building actions are needed to implement proposed reforms?

<--- Score

66. Are controls defined to recognize and contain problems?

<--- Score

67. Do you know what you need to know about Platform Positioning?

<--- Score

68. What information do users need?

<--- Score

69. Will it solve real problems?
<--- Score

70. Who needs to know about Platform Positioning?
<--- Score

71. What vendors make products that address the
Platform Positioning needs?
<--- Score

72. What resources or support might you need?
<--- Score

73. Are there Platform Positioning problems defined?
<--- Score

**74. What are your needs in relation to Platform
Positioning skills, labor, equipment, and markets?**
<--- Score

75. Did you miss any major Platform Positioning
issues?
<--- Score

76. How do you identify subcontractor relationships?
<--- Score

77. Think about the people you identified for
your Platform Positioning project and the project
responsibilities you would assign to them, what kind
of training do you think they would need to perform
these responsibilities effectively?
<--- Score

78. What is the smallest subset of the problem you

can usefully solve?
<--- Score

79. Are losses recognized in a timely manner?
<--- Score

80. What Platform Positioning capabilities do you need?
<--- Score

81. Who are your key stakeholders who need to sign off?
<--- Score

82. Where is training needed?
<--- Score

83. As a sponsor, customer or management, how important is it to meet goals, objectives?
<--- Score

84. How do you identify the kinds of information that you will need?
<--- Score

85. What problems are you facing and how do you consider Platform Positioning will circumvent those obstacles?
<--- Score

86. What extra resources will you need?
<--- Score

87. Is the need for organizational change recognized?
<--- Score

88. Will new equipment/products be required to facilitate Platform Positioning delivery, for example is new software needed?
<--- Score

89. What Platform Positioning problem should be solved?
<--- Score

90. Are employees recognized for desired behaviors?
<--- Score

91. What is the problem or issue?
<--- Score

92. Is it needed?
<--- Score

93. What are the expected benefits of Platform Positioning to the stakeholder?
<--- Score

94. Are there recognized Platform Positioning problems?
<--- Score

95. Is the quality assurance team identified?
<--- Score

Add up total points for this section:
_ _ _ _ _ = Total points for this section

Divided by: _ _ _ _ _ _ (number of statements answered) = _ _ _ _ _ _ Average score for this section

Transfer your score to the Platform Positioning Index at the beginning of the Self-Assessment.

CRITERION #2: DEFINE:

INTENT: Formulate the stakeholder problem. Define the problem, needs and objectives.

In my belief, the answer to this question is clearly defined:

5 Strongly Agree

4 Agree

3 Neutral

2 Disagree

1 Strongly Disagree

1. Has a team charter been developed and communicated?
<--- Score

2. How is the team tracking and documenting its work?
<--- Score

3. Are resources adequate for the scope?

<--- Score

4. Who is gathering information?
<--- Score

5. What was the context?
<--- Score

6. Is there any additional Platform Positioning definition of success?
<--- Score

7. Is there regularly 100% attendance at the team meetings? If not, have appointed substitutes attended to preserve cross-functionality and full representation?
<--- Score

8. What Platform Positioning services do you require?
<--- Score

9. What is in scope?
<--- Score

10. What is the scope of the Platform Positioning work?
<--- Score

11. Does the scope remain the same?
<--- Score

12. Where can you gather more information?
<--- Score

13. Are the Platform Positioning requirements testable?

<--- Score

14. When are meeting minutes sent out? Who is on the distribution list?
<--- Score

15. When is the estimated completion date?
<--- Score

16. How do you gather the stories?
<--- Score

17. Who is gathering Platform Positioning information?
<--- Score

18. Has/have the customer(s) been identified?
<--- Score

19. What are the Roles and Responsibilities for each team member and its leadership? Where is this documented?
<--- Score

20. How are consistent Platform Positioning definitions important?
<--- Score

21. How did the Platform Positioning manager receive input to the development of a Platform Positioning improvement plan and the estimated completion dates/times of each activity?
<--- Score

22. Is the Platform Positioning scope complete and appropriately sized?

<--- Score

23. In what way can you redefine the criteria of choice clients have in your category in your favor?
<--- Score

24. Has the direction changed at all during the course of Platform Positioning? If so, when did it change and why?
<--- Score

25. Has a high-level 'as is' process map been completed, verified and validated?
<--- Score

26. What are (control) requirements for Platform Positioning Information?
<--- Score

27. What are the Platform Positioning use cases?
<--- Score

28. Is there a clear Platform Positioning case definition?
<--- Score

29. What gets examined?
<--- Score

30. What is the definition of success?
<--- Score

31. How and when will the baselines be defined?
<--- Score

32. What key stakeholder process output measure(s)

does Platform Positioning leverage and how?
<--- Score

33. How will variation in the actual durations of each activity be dealt with to ensure that the expected Platform Positioning results are met?
<--- Score

34. What is the scope?
<--- Score

35. What specifically is the problem? Where does it occur? When does it occur? What is its extent?
<--- Score

36. What is a worst-case scenario for losses?
<--- Score

37. Are customer(s) identified and segmented according to their different needs and requirements?
<--- Score

38. The political context: who holds power?
<--- Score

39. Have specific policy objectives been defined?
<--- Score

40. How can the value of Platform Positioning be defined?
<--- Score

41. Do the problem and goal statements meet the SMART criteria (specific, measurable, attainable, relevant, and time-bound)?
<--- Score

42. Do you have a Platform Positioning success story or case study ready to tell and share?
<--- Score

43. How do you gather requirements?
<--- Score

44. Is there a completed, verified, and validated high-level 'as is' (not 'should be' or 'could be') stakeholder process map?
<--- Score

45. Is the work to date meeting requirements?
<--- Score

46. Is the team equipped with available and reliable resources?
<--- Score

47. What customer feedback methods were used to solicit their input?
<--- Score

48. How do you think the partners involved in Platform Positioning would have defined success?
<--- Score

49. What sort of initial information to gather?
<--- Score

50. If substitutes have been appointed, have they been briefed on the Platform Positioning goals and received regular communications as to the progress to date?
<--- Score

51. What are the rough order estimates on cost savings/opportunities that Platform Positioning brings?
<--- Score

52. What baselines are required to be defined and managed?
<--- Score

53. Are there different segments of customers?
<--- Score

54. How do you manage scope?
<--- Score

55. Is the team adequately staffed with the desired cross-functionality? If not, what additional resources are available to the team?
<--- Score

56. Are there any constraints known that bear on the ability to perform Platform Positioning work? How is the team addressing them?
<--- Score

57. How does the Platform Positioning manager ensure against scope creep?
<--- Score

58. Who are the Platform Positioning improvement team members, including Management Leads and Coaches?
<--- Score

59. Why are you doing Platform Positioning and

what is the scope?
<--- Score

60. What is out of scope?
<--- Score

61. Have all basic functions of Platform Positioning been defined?
<--- Score

62. What are the compelling stakeholder reasons for embarking on Platform Positioning?
<--- Score

63. Have the customer needs been translated into specific, measurable requirements? How?
<--- Score

64. What is the worst case scenario?
<--- Score

65. What are the core elements of the Platform Positioning business case?
<--- Score

66. Does the team have regular meetings?
<--- Score

67. Is there a completed SIPOC representation, describing the Suppliers, Inputs, Process, Outputs, and Customers?
<--- Score

68. What are the dynamics of the communication plan?
<--- Score

69. Is Platform Positioning currently on schedule according to the plan?
<--- Score

70. How would you define the culture at your organization, how susceptible is it to Platform Positioning changes?
<--- Score

71. How was the 'as is' process map developed, reviewed, verified and validated?
<--- Score

72. Scope of sensitive information?
<--- Score

73. Will a Platform Positioning production readiness review be required?
<--- Score

74. How do you hand over Platform Positioning context?
<--- Score

75. Who approved the Platform Positioning scope?
<--- Score

76. Do you all define Platform Positioning in the same way?
<--- Score

77. Is the current 'as is' process being followed? If not, what are the discrepancies?
<--- Score

78. Are approval levels defined for contracts and supplements to contracts?
<--- Score

79. Are task requirements clearly defined?
<--- Score

80. What critical content must be communicated – who, what, when, where, and how?
<--- Score

81. What scope do you want your strategy to cover?
<--- Score

82. What defines best in class?
<--- Score

83. Are the Platform Positioning requirements complete?
<--- Score

84. Is the scope of Platform Positioning defined?
<--- Score

85. When is/was the Platform Positioning start date?
<--- Score

86. What knowledge or experience is required?
<--- Score

87. Do you have organizational privacy requirements?
<--- Score

88. What are the Platform Positioning tasks and definitions?
<--- Score

89. Are required metrics defined, what are they?
<--- Score

90. Is the team formed and are team leaders (Coaches and Management Leads) assigned?
<--- Score

91. What scope to assess?
<--- Score

92. Who defines (or who defined) the rules and roles?
<--- Score

93. How do you gather Platform Positioning requirements?
<--- Score

94. What is the scope of Platform Positioning?
<--- Score

95. Is special Platform Positioning user knowledge required?
<--- Score

96. How often are the team meetings?
<--- Score

97. Has a project plan, Gantt chart, or similar been developed/completed?
<--- Score

98. How have you defined all Platform Positioning requirements first?
<--- Score

99. What constraints exist that might impact the team?
<--- Score

100. Are different versions of process maps needed to account for the different types of inputs?
<--- Score

101. How will the Platform Positioning team and the group measure complete success of Platform Positioning?
<--- Score

102. Is the Platform Positioning scope manageable?
<--- Score

103. How do you manage changes in Platform Positioning requirements?
<--- Score

104. What are the tasks and definitions?
<--- Score

105. Will team members regularly document their Platform Positioning work?
<--- Score

106. Is there a Platform Positioning management charter, including stakeholder case, problem and goal statements, scope, milestones, roles and responsibilities, communication plan?
<--- Score

107. Is scope creep really all bad news?
<--- Score

108. What Platform Positioning requirements should be gathered?
<--- Score

109. Has your scope been defined?
<--- Score

110. What are the boundaries of the scope? What is in bounds and what is not? What is the start point? What is the stop point?
<--- Score

111. Are all requirements met?
<--- Score

112. Has anyone else (internal or external to the group) attempted to solve this problem or a similar one before? If so, what knowledge can be leveraged from these previous efforts?
<--- Score

113. How do you build the right business case?
<--- Score

114. What are the requirements for audit information?
<--- Score

115. Are roles and responsibilities formally defined?
<--- Score

116. Are audit criteria, scope, frequency and methods defined?
<--- Score

117. What information should you gather?

<--- Score

118. Is Platform Positioning linked to key stakeholder goals and objectives?
<--- Score

119. Is the improvement team aware of the different versions of a process: what they think it is vs. what it actually is vs. what it should be vs. what it could be?
<--- Score

120. What is the context?
<--- Score

121. Is there a critical path to deliver Platform Positioning results?
<--- Score

122. How do you catch Platform Positioning definition inconsistencies?
<--- Score

123. Is Platform Positioning required?
<--- Score

124. Is full participation by members in regularly held team meetings guaranteed?
<--- Score

125. What system do you use for gathering Platform Positioning information?
<--- Score

126. How would you define Platform Positioning leadership?
<--- Score

127. What is the definition of Platform Positioning excellence?
<--- Score

128. Is data collected and displayed to better understand customer(s) critical needs and requirements.
<--- Score

129. Has the Platform Positioning work been fairly and/or equitably divided and delegated among team members who are qualified and capable to perform the work? Has everyone contributed?
<--- Score

130. Has everyone on the team, including the team leaders, been properly trained?
<--- Score

131. How do you keep key subject matter experts in the loop?
<--- Score

132. What would be the goal or target for a Platform Positioning's improvement team?
<--- Score

133. What is out-of-scope initially?
<--- Score

134. Are improvement team members fully trained on Platform Positioning?
<--- Score

135. Have all of the relationships been defined

properly?
<--- Score

136. What sources do you use to gather information for a Platform Positioning study?
<--- Score

137. What is the scope of the Platform Positioning effort?
<--- Score

138. Will team members perform Platform Positioning work when assigned and in a timely fashion?
<--- Score

139. Is it clearly defined in and to your organization what you do?
<--- Score

140. Has the improvement team collected the 'voice of the customer' (obtained feedback – qualitative and quantitative)?
<--- Score

Add up total points for this section:
_ _ _ _ _ = Total points for this section

Divided by: _ _ _ _ _ _ (number of statements answered) = _ _ _ _ _ _ Average score for this section

Transfer your score to the Platform Positioning Index at the beginning of the Self-Assessment.

CRITERION #3: MEASURE:

INTENT: Gather the correct data.
Measure the current performance and
evolution of the situation.

In my belief, the answer to this
question is clearly defined:

5 Strongly Agree

4 Agree

3 Neutral

2 Disagree

1 Strongly Disagree

1. What are the strategic priorities for this year?
<--- Score

2. Who should receive measurement reports?
<--- Score

3. What are the operational costs after Platform
Positioning deployment?
<--- Score

4. What does losing customers cost your organization?
<--- Score

5. Where can you go to verify the info?
<--- Score

6. Have you made assumptions about the shape of the future, particularly its impact on your customers and competitors?
<--- Score

7. How do you prevent mis-estimating cost?
<--- Score

8. How will effects be measured?
<--- Score

9. What is an unallowable cost?
<--- Score

10. How can you reduce the costs of obtaining inputs?
<--- Score

11. Why do the measurements/indicators matter?
<--- Score

12. At what cost?
<--- Score

13. How do you verify performance?
<--- Score

14. How do you quantify and qualify impacts?
<--- Score

15. Has a cost center been established?

<--- Score

16. How to cause the change?

<--- Score

17. How will your organization measure success?

<--- Score

18. When a disaster occurs, who gets priority?

<--- Score

19. Is the cost worth the Platform Positioning effort ?

<--- Score

20. Are the Platform Positioning benefits worth its costs?

<--- Score

21. Have design-to-cost goals been established?

<--- Score

22. Do you have any cost Platform Positioning limitation requirements?

<--- Score

23. What is the Platform Positioning business impact?

<--- Score

24. Are there competing Platform Positioning priorities?

<--- Score

25. What are the uncertainties surrounding estimates

of impact?

<--- Score

26. What evidence is there and what is measured?

<--- Score

27. Do you have a flow diagram of what happens?

<--- Score

28. Did you tackle the cause or the symptom?

<--- Score

29. What are hidden Platform Positioning quality costs?

<--- Score

30. What causes extra work or rework?

<--- Score

31. How can you measure Platform Positioning in a systematic way?

<--- Score

32. How long to keep data and how to manage retention costs?

<--- Score

33. Are you able to realize any cost savings?

<--- Score

34. How do you verify the authenticity of the data and information used?

<--- Score

35. What causes innovation to fail or succeed in your organization?

<--- Score

36. What measurements are possible, practicable and meaningful?
<--- Score

37. What do people want to verify?
<--- Score

38. How do you control the overall costs of your work processes?
<--- Score

39. What is your Platform Positioning quality cost segregation study?
<--- Score

40. What is your decision requirements diagram?
<--- Score

41. Where is it measured?
<--- Score

42. How do you verify and develop ideas and innovations?
<--- Score

43. How do you measure efficient delivery of Platform Positioning services?
<--- Score

44. How do you verify and validate the Platform Positioning data?
<--- Score

45. What are the estimated costs of proposed

changes?

<--- Score

46. What are the current costs of the Platform Positioning process?

<--- Score

47. What harm might be caused?

<--- Score

48. Are supply costs steady or fluctuating?

<--- Score

49. Where is the cost?

<--- Score

50. How do you verify if Platform Positioning is built right?

<--- Score

51. How frequently do you track Platform Positioning measures?

<--- Score

52. How do you aggregate measures across priorities?

<--- Score

53. What could cause delays in the schedule?

<--- Score

54. When should you bother with diagrams?

<--- Score

55. How are measurements made?

<--- Score

56. Do you verify that corrective actions were taken?

<--- Score

57. How will success or failure be measured?

<--- Score

58. Which costs should be taken into account?

<--- Score

59. Which Platform Positioning impacts are significant?

<--- Score

60. What is the cost of rework?

<--- Score

61. How do you measure variability?

<--- Score

62. What measurements are being captured?

<--- Score

63. What potential environmental factors impact the Platform Positioning effort?

<--- Score

64. Are Platform Positioning vulnerabilities categorized and prioritized?

<--- Score

65. How can you reduce costs?

<--- Score

66. Who pays the cost?

<--- Score

67. Are there any easy-to-implement alternatives to Platform Positioning? Sometimes other solutions are available that do not require the cost implications of a full-blown project?

<--- Score

68. What are you verifying?

<--- Score

69. What is the root cause(s) of the problem?

<--- Score

70. What are the costs of delaying Platform Positioning action?

<--- Score

71. What are your primary costs, revenues, assets?

<--- Score

72. Is there an opportunity to verify requirements?

<--- Score

73. How can a Platform Positioning test verify your ideas or assumptions?

<--- Score

74. How will measures be used to manage and adapt?

<--- Score

75. What is measured? Why?

<--- Score

76. Which measures and indicators matter?

<--- Score

77. Do you effectively measure and reward individual and team performance?
<--- Score

78. What disadvantage does this cause for the user?
<--- Score

79. What would be a real cause for concern?
<--- Score

80. How do you measure lifecycle phases?
<--- Score

81. How do you measure success?
<--- Score

82. How do your measurements capture actionable Platform Positioning information for use in exceeding your customers expectations and securing your customers engagement?
<--- Score

83. What is the total cost related to deploying Platform Positioning, including any consulting or professional services?
<--- Score

84. What are allowable costs?
<--- Score

85. What could cause you to change course?
<--- Score

86. What are your operating costs?
<--- Score

87. Do you aggressively reward and promote the people who have the biggest impact on creating excellent Platform Positioning services/products?
<--- Score

88. What users will be impacted?
<--- Score

89. What happens if cost savings do not materialize?
<--- Score

90. Is the solution cost-effective?
<--- Score

91. When are costs are incurred?
<--- Score

92. How do you verify the Platform Positioning requirements quality?
<--- Score

93. Do the benefits outweigh the costs?
<--- Score

94. What details are required of the Platform Positioning cost structure?
<--- Score

95. How can you measure the performance?
<--- Score

96. Are actual costs in line with budgeted costs?
<--- Score

97. How do you verify your resources?
<--- Score

98. Is it possible to estimate the impact of unanticipated complexity such as wrong or failed assumptions, feedback, etcetera on proposed reforms?

<--- Score

99. What are your key Platform Positioning organizational performance measures, including key short and longer-term financial measures?

<--- Score

100. What is the total fixed cost?

<--- Score

101. What causes mismanagement?

<--- Score

102. What are the costs of reform?

<--- Score

103. How is the value delivered by Platform Positioning being measured?

<--- Score

104. What are the Platform Positioning key cost drivers?

<--- Score

105. Does management have the right priorities among projects?

<--- Score

106. Are you aware of what could cause a problem?

<--- Score

107. What can be used to verify compliance?
<--- Score

108. Are the measurements objective?
<--- Score

109. How will costs be allocated?
<--- Score

110. How is performance measured?
<--- Score

111. What causes investor action?
<--- Score

112. Are missed Platform Positioning opportunities costing your organization money?
<--- Score

113. Have you included everything in your Platform Positioning cost models?
<--- Score

114. What are your customers expectations and measures?
<--- Score

115. What are the Platform Positioning investment costs?
<--- Score

116. How sensitive must the Platform Positioning strategy be to cost?
<--- Score

117. Does a Platform Positioning quantification method exist?
<--- Score

118. What are the costs and benefits?
<--- Score

119. Do you have an issue in getting priority?
<--- Score

120. What does a Test Case verify?
<--- Score

121. Will Platform Positioning have an impact on current business continuity, disaster recovery processes and/or infrastructure?
<--- Score

122. What drives O&M cost?
<--- Score

123. What are the costs?
<--- Score

124. Why do you expend time and effort to implement measurement, for whom?
<--- Score

125. How will you measure success?
<--- Score

126. What would it cost to replace your technology?
<--- Score

127. How much does it cost?
<--- Score

128. Was a business case (cost/benefit) developed?
<--- Score

129. Are you taking your company in the direction of better and revenue or cheaper and cost?
<--- Score

130. How are costs allocated?
<--- Score

131. What tests verify requirements?
<--- Score

132. Are there measurements based on task performance?
<--- Score

133. What do you measure and why?
<--- Score

134. What relevant entities could be measured?
<--- Score

135. Does the Platform Positioning task fit the client's priorities?
<--- Score

136. How can you manage cost down?
<--- Score

137. Who is involved in verifying compliance?
<--- Score

138. How will you measure your Platform Positioning effectiveness?

<--- Score

139. What does your operating model cost?
<--- Score

140. Among the Platform Positioning product and service cost to be estimated, which is considered hardest to estimate?
<--- Score

141. What are the types and number of measures to use?
<--- Score

142. Are indirect costs charged to the Platform Positioning program?
<--- Score

Add up total points for this section:
_ _ _ _ _ = Total points for this section

Divided by: _ _ _ _ _ _ (number of statements answered) = _ _ _ _ _ _
Average score for this section

Transfer your score to the Platform Positioning Index at the beginning of the Self-Assessment.

CRITERION #4: ANALYZE:

1. How do you use Platform Positioning data and information to support organizational decision making and innovation?
<--- Score

2. Were Pareto charts (or similar) used to portray the 'heavy hitters' (or key sources of variation)?
<--- Score

3. What other jobs or tasks affect the performance

of the steps in the Platform Positioning process?
<--- Score

4. What quality tools were used to get through the analyze phase?
<--- Score

5. What are your Platform Positioning processes?
<--- Score

6. Record-keeping requirements flow from the records needed as inputs, outputs, controls and for transformation of a Platform Positioning process, are the records needed as inputs to the Platform Positioning process available?
<--- Score

7. How do you measure the operational performance of your key work systems and processes, including productivity, cycle time, and other appropriate measures of process effectiveness, efficiency, and innovation?
<--- Score

8. Think about the functions involved in your Platform Positioning project, what processes flow from these functions?
<--- Score

9. How is the way you as the leader think and process information affecting your organizational culture?
<--- Score

10. What are the revised rough estimates of the financial savings/opportunity for Platform Positioning

improvements?

<--- Score

11. How has the Platform Positioning data been gathered?

<--- Score

12. What types of data do your Platform Positioning indicators require?

<--- Score

13. What are the necessary qualifications?

<--- Score

14. Do you understand your management processes today?

<--- Score

15. What are the processes for audit reporting and management?

<--- Score

16. What Platform Positioning metrics are outputs of the process?

<--- Score

17. What are evaluation criteria for the output?

<--- Score

18. When should a process be art not science?

<--- Score

19. What tools were used to generate the list of possible causes?

<--- Score

20. What information qualified as important?

<--- Score

21. Do staff qualifications match your project?

<--- Score

22. What did the team gain from developing a sub-process map?

<--- Score

23. What are your key performance measures or indicators and in-process measures for the control and improvement of your Platform Positioning processes?

<--- Score

24. What do you need to qualify?

<--- Score

25. What data is gathered?

<--- Score

26. Are your outputs consistent?

<--- Score

27. What qualifications do Platform Positioning leaders need?

<--- Score

28. Is the performance gap determined?

<--- Score

29. Who will facilitate the team and process?

<--- Score

30. Has an output goal been set?

<--- Score

31. Who qualifies to gain access to data?
<--- Score

32. What qualifies as competition?
<--- Score

33. What Platform Positioning data should be managed?
<--- Score

34. What were the financial benefits resulting from any 'ground fruit or low-hanging fruit' (quick fixes)?
<--- Score

35. What other organizational variables, such as reward systems or communication systems, affect the performance of this Platform Positioning process?
<--- Score

36. How much data can be collected in the given timeframe?
<--- Score

37. What is the cost of poor quality as supported by the team's analysis?
<--- Score

38. What resources go in to get the desired output?
<--- Score

39. What are the Platform Positioning design outputs?
<--- Score

40. Do several people in different organizational units

assist with the Platform Positioning process?
<--- Score

41. How does the organization define, manage, and improve its Platform Positioning processes?
<--- Score

42. A compounding model resolution with available relevant data can often provide insight towards a solution methodology; which Platform Positioning models, tools and techniques are necessary?
<--- Score

43. What process improvements will be needed?
<--- Score

44. What Platform Positioning data do you gather or use now?
<--- Score

45. What is the complexity of the output produced?
<--- Score

46. An organizationally feasible system request is one that considers the mission, goals and objectives of the organization, key questions are: is the Platform Positioning solution request practical and will it solve a problem or take advantage of an opportunity to achieve company goals?
<--- Score

47. How many input/output points does it require?
<--- Score

48. Where is the data coming from to measure

compliance?
<--- Score

49. What is the oversight process?
<--- Score

50. What is your organizations system for selecting qualified vendors?
<--- Score

51. What data do you need to collect?
<--- Score

52. How will corresponding data be collected?
<--- Score

53. Is the gap/opportunity displayed and communicated in financial terms?
<--- Score

54. Do you have the authority to produce the output?
<--- Score

55. Is pre-qualification of suppliers carried out?
<--- Score

56. Were there any improvement opportunities identified from the process analysis?
<--- Score

57. How will the change process be managed?
<--- Score

58. What are your best practices for minimizing Platform Positioning project risk, while demonstrating incremental value and quick wins throughout the

Platform Positioning project lifecycle?
<--- Score

59. What tools were used to narrow the list of possible causes?
<--- Score

60. Was a detailed process map created to amplify critical steps of the 'as is' stakeholder process?
<--- Score

61. What Platform Positioning data should be collected?
<--- Score

62. How do you identify specific Platform Positioning investment opportunities and emerging trends?
<--- Score

63. What are your current levels and trends in key measures or indicators of Platform Positioning product and process performance that are important to and directly serve your customers? How do these results compare with the performance of your competitors and other organizations with similar offerings?
<--- Score

64. How do you ensure that the Platform Positioning opportunity is realistic?
<--- Score

65. What will drive Platform Positioning change?
<--- Score

66. How is the Platform Positioning Value Stream Mapping managed?
<--- Score

67. Do your employees have the opportunity to do what they do best everyday?
<--- Score

68. How do your work systems and key work processes relate to and capitalize on your core competencies?
<--- Score

69. How often will data be collected for measures?
<--- Score

70. Are all staff in core Platform Positioning subjects Highly Qualified?
<--- Score

71. Were any designed experiments used to generate additional insight into the data analysis?
<--- Score

72. Where is Platform Positioning data gathered?
<--- Score

73. What is the output?
<--- Score

74. Who gets your output?
<--- Score

75. What are your current levels and trends in key Platform Positioning measures or indicators of product and process performance that are important

to and directly serve your customers?
<--- Score

76. What is the Platform Positioning Driver?
<--- Score

77. What are the best opportunities for value improvement?
<--- Score

78. What were the crucial 'moments of truth' on the process map?
<--- Score

79. What are the personnel training and qualifications required?
<--- Score

80. What does the data say about the performance of the stakeholder process?
<--- Score

81. What qualifications are needed?
<--- Score

82. What conclusions were drawn from the team's data collection and analysis? How did the team reach these conclusions?
<--- Score

83. What is your organizations process which leads to recognition of value generation?
<--- Score

84. How will the Platform Positioning data be captured?

<--- Score

85. What Platform Positioning data will be collected?
<--- Score

86. Who owns what data?
<--- Score

87. What successful thing are you doing today that may be blinding you to new growth opportunities?
<--- Score

88. What are the Platform Positioning business drivers?
<--- Score

89. How do you define collaboration and team output?
<--- Score

90. Identify an operational issue in your organization, for example, could a particular task be done more quickly or more efficiently by Platform Positioning?
<--- Score

91. Is there an established change management process?
<--- Score

92. What is the Value Stream Mapping?
<--- Score

93. Is the required Platform Positioning data gathered?
<--- Score

94. How are outputs preserved and protected?
<--- Score

95. Are all team members qualified for all tasks?
<--- Score

96. Which Platform Positioning data should be retained?
<--- Score

97. Was a cause-and-effect diagram used to explore the different types of causes (or sources of variation)?
<--- Score

98. What qualifications are necessary?
<--- Score

99. Think about some of the processes you undertake within your organization, which do you own?
<--- Score

100. What internal processes need improvement?
<--- Score

101. What training and qualifications will you need?
<--- Score

102. Is the suppliers process defined and controlled?
<--- Score

103. What qualifications and skills do you need?
<--- Score

104. How is data used for program management and

improvement?

<--- Score

105. Should you invest in industry-recognized qualifications?

<--- Score

106. What kind of crime could a potential new hire have committed that would not only not disqualify him/her from being hired by your organization, but would actually indicate that he/she might be a particularly good fit?

<--- Score

107. How difficult is it to qualify what Platform Positioning ROI is?

<--- Score

108. Where can you get qualified talent today?

<--- Score

109. How can risk management be tied procedurally to process elements?

<--- Score

110. What output to create?

<--- Score

111. What, related to, Platform Positioning processes does your organization outsource?

<--- Score

112. Can you add value to the current Platform Positioning decision-making process (largely qualitative) by incorporating uncertainty modeling (more quantitative)?

<--- Score

113. Who is involved with workflow mapping?
<--- Score

114. Are Platform Positioning changes recognized early enough to be approved through the regular process?
<--- Score

115. How will the data be checked for quality?
<--- Score

116. Has data output been validated?
<--- Score

117. How is Platform Positioning data gathered?
<--- Score

118. What are the disruptive Platform Positioning technologies that enable your organization to radically change your business processes?
<--- Score

119. What controls do you have in place to protect data?
<--- Score

120. Is the Platform Positioning process severely broken such that a re-design is necessary?
<--- Score

121. Do you, as a leader, bounce back quickly from setbacks?
<--- Score

122. Have you defined which data is gathered how?
<--- Score

123. Do quality systems drive continuous improvement?
<--- Score

124. Is the final output clearly identified?
<--- Score

125. What are your outputs?
<--- Score

126. Do your leaders quickly bounce back from setbacks?
<--- Score

127. What methods do you use to gather Platform Positioning data?
<--- Score

128. Are you missing Platform Positioning opportunities?
<--- Score

129. How is the data gathered?
<--- Score

130. How do you implement and manage your work processes to ensure that they meet design requirements?
<--- Score

131. Is there a strict change management process?
<--- Score

Add up total points for this section:

_____ = Total points for this section

Divided by: _____ (number of statements answered) = _____ Average score for this section

Transfer your score to the Platform Positioning Index at the beginning of the Self-Assessment.

CRITERION #5: IMPROVE:

INTENT: Develop a practical solution. Innovate, establish and test the solution and to measure the results.

In my belief, the answer to this question is clearly defined:

5 Strongly Agree

4 Agree

3 Neutral

2 Disagree

1 Strongly Disagree

1. What are your current levels and trends in key measures or indicators of workforce and leader development?
<--- Score

2. Are the risks fully understood, reasonable and manageable?
<--- Score

3. How do you measure risk?

<--- Score

4. Who makes the Platform Positioning decisions in your organization?

<--- Score

5. Who will be responsible for making the decisions to include or exclude requested changes once Platform Positioning is underway?

<--- Score

6. If you could go back in time five years, what decision would you make differently? What is your best guess as to what decision you're making today you might regret five years from now?

<--- Score

7. What communications are necessary to support the implementation of the solution?

<--- Score

8. Was a Platform Positioning charter developed?

<--- Score

9. Have you identified breakpoints and/or risk tolerances that will trigger broad consideration of a potential need for intervention or modification of strategy?

<--- Score

10. How do you deal with Platform Positioning risk?

<--- Score

11. Can you integrate quality management and risk management?

<--- Score

12. What can you do to improve?
<--- Score

13. Which of the recognised risks out of all risks can be most likely transferred?
<--- Score

14. What attendant changes will need to be made to ensure that the solution is successful?
<--- Score

15. Does a good decision guarantee a good outcome?
<--- Score

16. How can you improve performance?
<--- Score

17. What is Platform Positioning risk?
<--- Score

18. Do you need to do a usability evaluation?
<--- Score

19. What tools were used to tap into the creativity and encourage 'outside the box' thinking?
<--- Score

20. What are the affordable Platform Positioning risks?
<--- Score

21. Risk factors: what are the characteristics of Platform Positioning that make it risky?
<--- Score

22. Is there a small-scale pilot for proposed improvement(s)? What conclusions were drawn from the outcomes of a pilot?
<--- Score

23. What assumptions are made about the solution and approach?
<--- Score

24. How do you measure improved Platform Positioning service perception, and satisfaction?
<--- Score

25. What to do with the results or outcomes of measurements?
<--- Score

26. What tools do you use once you have decided on a Platform Positioning strategy and more importantly how do you choose?
<--- Score

27. Is the Platform Positioning documentation thorough?
<--- Score

28. How do the Platform Positioning results compare with the performance of your competitors and other organizations with similar offerings?
<--- Score

29. Is the solution technically practical?
<--- Score

30. What tools were used to evaluate the potential solutions?

<--- Score

31. How will you know when its improved?
<--- Score

32. What is the Platform Positioning's sustainability risk?
<--- Score

33. When you map the key players in your own work and the types/domains of relationships with them, which relationships do you find easy and which challenging, and why?
<--- Score

34. What strategies for Platform Positioning improvement are successful?
<--- Score

35. Where do you need Platform Positioning improvement?
<--- Score

36. How do you improve Platform Positioning service perception, and satisfaction?
<--- Score

37. Will the controls trigger any other risks?
<--- Score

38. Is there a high likelihood that any recommendations will achieve their intended results?
<--- Score

39. How do you mitigate Platform Positioning risk?
<--- Score

40. Who do you report Platform Positioning results to?
<--- Score

41. Who controls the risk?
<--- Score

42. How will you recognize and celebrate results?
<--- Score

43. For estimation problems, how do you develop an estimation statement?
<--- Score

44. How do you decide how much to remunerate an employee?
<--- Score

45. What practices helps your organization to develop its capacity to recognize patterns?
<--- Score

46. Do you cover the five essential competencies: Communication, Collaboration,Innovation, Adaptability, and Leadership that improve an organizations ability to leverage the new Platform Positioning in a volatile global economy?
<--- Score

47. Who are the Platform Positioning decision makers?
<--- Score

48. What Platform Positioning improvements can be made?
<--- Score

49. What tools were most useful during the improve phase?
<--- Score

50. Who manages Platform Positioning risk?
<--- Score

51. How will you measure the results?
<--- Score

52. Who will be using the results of the measurement activities?
<--- Score

53. How scalable is your Platform Positioning solution?
<--- Score

54. How do you manage Platform Positioning risk?
<--- Score

55. Are you assessing Platform Positioning and risk?
<--- Score

56. Are events managed to resolution?
<--- Score

57. Are procedures documented for managing Platform Positioning risks?
<--- Score

58. What is Platform Positioning's impact on utilizing the best solution(s)?
<--- Score

59. Have you achieved Platform Positioning

improvements?
<--- Score

60. What were the underlying assumptions on the cost-benefit analysis?
<--- Score

61. What are the expected Platform Positioning results?
<--- Score

62. Are risk management tasks balanced centrally and locally?
<--- Score

63. Who are the key stakeholders for the Platform Positioning evaluation?
<--- Score

64. Who controls key decisions that will be made?
<--- Score

65. Was a pilot designed for the proposed solution(s)?
<--- Score

66. What error proofing will be done to address some of the discrepancies observed in the 'as is' process?
<--- Score

67. How are policy decisions made and where?
<--- Score

68. Risk events: what are the things that could go wrong?
<--- Score

69. What are the implications of the one critical Platform Positioning decision 10 minutes, 10 months, and 10 years from now?
<--- Score

70. Which Platform Positioning solution is appropriate?
<--- Score

71. How can skill-level changes improve Platform Positioning?
<--- Score

72. How do you improve productivity?
<--- Score

73. Do you have the optimal project management team structure?
<--- Score

74. In the past few months, what is the smallest change you have made that has had the biggest positive result? What was it about that small change that produced the large return?
<--- Score

75. How can you improve Platform Positioning?
<--- Score

76. What resources are required for the improvement efforts?
<--- Score

77. What lessons, if any, from a pilot were incorporated into the design of the full-scale solution?
<--- Score

78. What should a proof of concept or pilot accomplish?
<--- Score

79. Would you develop a Platform Positioning Communication Strategy?
<--- Score

80. How does your organization evaluate strategic Platform Positioning success?
<--- Score

81. What are the concrete Platform Positioning results?
<--- Score

82. Is there any other Platform Positioning solution?
<--- Score

83. What improvements have been achieved?
<--- Score

84. Risk Identification: What are the possible risk events your organization faces in relation to Platform Positioning?
<--- Score

85. How does the team improve its work?
<--- Score

86. How can you better manage risk?
<--- Score

87. How is continuous improvement applied to risk management?

<--- Score

88. How do you define the solutions' scope?
<--- Score

89. How will you know that a change is an improvement?
<--- Score

90. Who will be responsible for documenting the Platform Positioning requirements in detail?
<--- Score

91. Is risk periodically assessed?
<--- Score

92. Is the scope clearly documented?
<--- Score

93. Where do the Platform Positioning decisions reside?
<--- Score

94. Who are the people involved in developing and implementing Platform Positioning?
<--- Score

95. Is supporting Platform Positioning documentation required?
<--- Score

96. How risky is your organization?
<--- Score

97. What is the team's contingency plan for potential problems occurring in implementation?

<--- Score

98. What is the implementation plan?
<--- Score

99. How do you manage and improve your Platform Positioning work systems to deliver customer value and achieve organizational success and sustainability?
<--- Score

100. At what point will vulnerability assessments be performed once Platform Positioning is put into production (e.g., ongoing Risk Management after implementation)?
<--- Score

101. What is the magnitude of the improvements?
<--- Score

102. Is any Platform Positioning documentation required?
<--- Score

103. What does the 'should be' process map/design look like?
<--- Score

104. How do you go about comparing Platform Positioning approaches/solutions?
<--- Score

105. Were any criteria developed to assist the team in testing and evaluating potential solutions?
<--- Score

106. Do those selected for the Platform Positioning team have a good general understanding of what Platform Positioning is all about?
<--- Score

107. Are the most efficient solutions problem-specific?
<--- Score

108. To what extent does management recognize Platform Positioning as a tool to increase the results?
<--- Score

109. How do you improve your likelihood of success ?
<--- Score

110. Are decisions made in a timely manner?
<--- Score

111. What is the risk?
<--- Score

112. Is the measure of success for Platform Positioning understandable to a variety of people?
<--- Score

113. Is there a cost/benefit analysis of optimal solution(s)?
<--- Score

114. How will you know that you have improved?
<--- Score

115. Platform Positioning risk decisions: whose call Is It?
<--- Score

116. Who should make the Platform Positioning decisions?

<--- Score

117. Who manages supplier risk management in your organization?

<--- Score

118. How are Platform Positioning risks managed?

<--- Score

119. Are risk triggers captured?

<--- Score

120. What area needs the greatest improvement?

<--- Score

121. What were the criteria for evaluating a Platform Positioning pilot?

<--- Score

122. What went well, what should change, what can improve?

<--- Score

123. What actually has to improve and by how much?

<--- Score

124. Who are the Platform Positioning decision-makers?

<--- Score

125. How do you link measurement and risk?

<--- Score

126. Can you identify any significant risks or exposures to Platform Positioning third- parties (vendors, service providers, alliance partners etc) that concern you?
<--- Score

127. How can the phases of Platform Positioning development be identified?
<--- Score

128. How do you keep improving Platform Positioning?
<--- Score

129. What criteria will you use to assess your Platform Positioning risks?
<--- Score

130. Is the Platform Positioning risk managed?
<--- Score

131. How do you measure progress and evaluate training effectiveness?
<--- Score

132. Do you combine technical expertise with business knowledge and Platform Positioning Key topics include lifecycles, development approaches, requirements and how to make a business case?
<--- Score

Add up total points for this section:
_ _ _ _ _ = Total points for this section

Divided by: _ _ _ _ _ _ (number of statements answered) = _ _ _ _ _ _
Average score for this section

Transfer your score to the Platform
Positioning Index at the beginning of
the Self-Assessment.

CRITERION #6: CONTROL:

INTENT: Implement the practical
solution. Maintain the performance and
correct possible complications.

In my belief, the answer to this
question is clearly defined:

5 Strongly Agree

4 Agree

3 Neutral

2 Disagree

1 Strongly Disagree

1. Are controls in place and consistently applied?
<--- Score

2. Are you measuring, monitoring and predicting
Platform Positioning activities to optimize operations
and profitability, and enhancing outcomes?
<--- Score

3. Is there a recommended audit plan for routine

surveillance inspections of Platform Positioning's gains?
<--- Score

4. What is the best design framework for Platform Positioning organization now that, in a post industrial-age if the top-down, command and control model is no longer relevant?
<--- Score

5. Who will be in control?
<--- Score

6. What are the critical parameters to watch?
<--- Score

7. Act/Adjust: What Do you Need to Do Differently?
<--- Score

8. How do you plan for the cost of succession?
<--- Score

9. Who sets the Platform Positioning standards?
<--- Score

10. How do controls support value?
<--- Score

11. You may have created your quality measures at a time when you lacked resources, technology wasn't up to the required standard, or low service levels were the industry norm. Have those circumstances changed?
<--- Score

12. How do you monitor usage and cost?

<--- Score

13. What is the control/monitoring plan?
<--- Score

14. Will your goals reflect your program budget?
<--- Score

15. Who has control over resources?
<--- Score

16. Will the team be available to assist members in planning investigations?
<--- Score

17. Is there an action plan in case of emergencies?
<--- Score

18. Do the Platform Positioning decisions you make today help people and the planet tomorrow?
<--- Score

19. What key inputs and outputs are being measured on an ongoing basis?
<--- Score

20. How can you best use all of your knowledge repositories to enhance learning and sharing?
<--- Score

21. How will report readings be checked to effectively monitor performance?
<--- Score

22. Do you monitor the effectiveness of your Platform Positioning activities?

<--- Score

23. Will any special training be provided for results interpretation?
<--- Score

24. Is new knowledge gained imbedded in the response plan?
<--- Score

25. What Platform Positioning standards are applicable?
<--- Score

26. Is knowledge gained on process shared and institutionalized?
<--- Score

27. How do you establish and deploy modified action plans if circumstances require a shift in plans and rapid execution of new plans?
<--- Score

28. Is there documentation that will support the successful operation of the improvement?
<--- Score

29. How do your controls stack up?
<--- Score

30. What are the known security controls?
<--- Score

31. How will the process owner and team be able to hold the gains?
<--- Score

32. Are operating procedures consistent?
<--- Score

33. How will the process owner verify improvement in present and future sigma levels, process capabilities?
<--- Score

34. Does job training on the documented procedures need to be part of the process team's education and training?
<--- Score

35. What quality tools were useful in the control phase?
<--- Score

36. How widespread is its use?
<--- Score

37. What other systems, operations, processes, and infrastructures (hiring practices, staffing, training, incentives/rewards, metrics/dashboards/scorecards, etc.) need updates, additions, changes, or deletions in order to facilitate knowledge transfer and improvements?
<--- Score

38. Where do ideas that reach policy makers and planners as proposals for Platform Positioning strengthening and reform actually originate?
<--- Score

39. Who is going to spread your message?
<--- Score

40. Will existing staff require re-training, for example, to learn new business processes?
<--- Score

41. What should the next improvement project be that is related to Platform Positioning?
<--- Score

42. How do you select, collect, align, and integrate Platform Positioning data and information for tracking daily operations and overall organizational performance, including progress relative to strategic objectives and action plans?
<--- Score

43. Is there a control plan in place for sustaining improvements (short and long-term)?
<--- Score

44. How do you spread information?
<--- Score

45. What do you measure to verify effectiveness gains?
<--- Score

46. How do you plan on providing proper recognition and disclosure of supporting companies?
<--- Score

47. Are new process steps, standards, and documentation ingrained into normal operations?
<--- Score

48. Do you monitor the Platform Positioning decisions made and fine tune them as they evolve?

<--- Score

49. What are customers monitoring?
<--- Score

50. Does the Platform Positioning performance meet the customer's requirements?
<--- Score

51. What adjustments to the strategies are needed?
<--- Score

52. Does a troubleshooting guide exist or is it needed?
<--- Score

53. Is there a documented and implemented monitoring plan?
<--- Score

54. How is change control managed?
<--- Score

55. Is there a Platform Positioning Communication plan covering who needs to get what information when?
<--- Score

56. Who is the Platform Positioning process owner?
<--- Score

57. Are suggested corrective/restorative actions indicated on the response plan for known causes to problems that might surface?
<--- Score

58. Is reporting being used or needed?

<--- Score

59. What is your theory of human motivation, and how does your compensation plan fit with that view?
<--- Score

60. Is a response plan in place for when the input, process, or output measures indicate an 'out-of-control' condition?
<--- Score

61. What is your plan to assess your security risks?
<--- Score

62. How will new or emerging customer needs/requirements be checked/communicated to orient the process toward meeting the new specifications and continually reducing variation?
<--- Score

63. Is there a transfer of ownership and knowledge to process owner and process team tasked with the responsibilities.
<--- Score

64. Has the improved process and its steps been standardized?
<--- Score

65. Is a response plan established and deployed?
<--- Score

66. What is the recommended frequency of auditing?
<--- Score

67. Does the response plan contain a definite closed

loop continual improvement scheme (e.g., plan-do-check-act)?

<--- Score

68. How might the group capture best practices and lessons learned so as to leverage improvements?

<--- Score

69. What is the standard for acceptable Platform Positioning performance?

<--- Score

70. Are the planned controls working?

<--- Score

71. Against what alternative is success being measured?

<--- Score

72. Is there a standardized process?

<--- Score

73. What should you measure to verify efficiency gains?

<--- Score

74. Implementation Planning: is a pilot needed to test the changes before a full roll out occurs?

<--- Score

75. Are documented procedures clear and easy to follow for the operators?

<--- Score

76. How is Platform Positioning project cost planned, managed, monitored?

<--- Score

77. How do you encourage people to take control and responsibility?
<--- Score

78. How do senior leaders actions reflect a commitment to the organizations Platform Positioning values?
<--- Score

79. Who controls critical resources?
<--- Score

80. Are the planned controls in place?
<--- Score

81. What other areas of the group might benefit from the Platform Positioning team's improvements, knowledge, and learning?
<--- Score

82. What can you control?
<--- Score

83. What are the key elements of your Platform Positioning performance improvement system, including your evaluation, organizational learning, and innovation processes?
<--- Score

84. What do your reports reflect?
<--- Score

85. How likely is the current Platform Positioning plan to come in on schedule or on budget?

<--- Score

86. How will you measure your QA plan's effectiveness?
<--- Score

87. Can support from partners be adjusted?
<--- Score

88. How will the day-to-day responsibilities for monitoring and continual improvement be transferred from the improvement team to the process owner?
<--- Score

89. Can you adapt and adjust to changing Platform Positioning situations?
<--- Score

90. Are the Platform Positioning standards challenging?
<--- Score

91. How will input, process, and output variables be checked to detect for sub-optimal conditions?
<--- Score

92. What are you attempting to measure/monitor?
<--- Score

93. What do you stand for--and what are you against?
<--- Score

94. Have new or revised work instructions resulted?
<--- Score

95. What are your results for key measures or indicators of the accomplishment of your Platform Positioning strategy and action plans, including building and strengthening core competencies?
<--- Score

96. Is the Platform Positioning test/monitoring cost justified?
<--- Score

97. Has the Platform Positioning value of standards been quantified?
<--- Score

98. Are there documented procedures?
<--- Score

Add up total points for this section:
_ _ _ _ _ = Total points for this section

Divided by: _ _ _ _ _ _ (number of statements answered) = _ _ _ _ _ _
Average score for this section

Transfer your score to the Platform Positioning Index at the beginning of the Self-Assessment.

CRITERION #7: SUSTAIN:

INTENT: Retain the benefits.

In my belief, the answer to this question is clearly defined:

5 Strongly Agree

4 Agree

3 Neutral

2 Disagree

1 Strongly Disagree

1. How do you determine the key elements that affect Platform Positioning workforce satisfaction, how are these elements determined for different workforce groups and segments?
<--- Score

2. Are you using a design thinking approach and integrating Innovation, Platform Positioning Experience, and Brand Value?
<--- Score

3. Who is on the team?
<--- Score

4. How do you stay inspired?
<--- Score

5. Do you think Platform Positioning accomplishes the goals you expect it to accomplish?
<--- Score

6. Whose voice (department, ethnic group, women, older workers, etc) might you have missed hearing from in your company, and how might you amplify this voice to create positive momentum for your business?
<--- Score

7. In retrospect, of the projects that you pulled the plug on, what percent do you wish had been allowed to keep going, and what percent do you wish had ended earlier?
<--- Score

8. Is Platform Positioning realistic, or are you setting yourself up for failure?
<--- Score

9. How do you transition from the baseline to the target?
<--- Score

10. What are your most important goals for the strategic Platform Positioning objectives?
<--- Score

11. What trouble can you get into?

<--- Score

12. What is an unauthorized commitment?
<--- Score

13. Are you paying enough attention to the partners your company depends on to succeed?
<--- Score

14. What happens if you do not have enough funding?
<--- Score

15. How will you motivate the stakeholders with the least vested interest?
<--- Score

16. Who else should you help?
<--- Score

17. How do you ensure that implementations of Platform Positioning products are done in a way that ensures safety?
<--- Score

18. What is your question? Why?
<--- Score

19. When information truly is ubiquitous, when reach and connectivity are completely global, when computing resources are infinite, and when a whole new set of impossibilities are not only possible, but happening, what will that do to your business?
<--- Score

20. How is implementation research currently incorporated into each of your goals?
<--- Score

21. What happens at your organization when people fail?
<--- Score

22. How important is Platform Positioning to the user organizations mission?
<--- Score

23. What is the overall business strategy?
<--- Score

24. What potential megatrends could make your business model obsolete?
<--- Score

25. What relationships among Platform Positioning trends do you perceive?
<--- Score

26. Who will manage the integration of tools?
<--- Score

27. What stupid rule would you most like to kill?
<--- Score

28. What unique value proposition (UVP) do you offer?
<--- Score

29. How can you negotiate Platform Positioning successfully with a stubborn boss, an irate client, or a deceitful coworker?
<--- Score

30. Do you feel that more should be done in the Platform Positioning area?
<--- Score

31. What Platform Positioning modifications can you make work for you?
<--- Score

32. How do you keep records, of what?
<--- Score

33. Whom among your colleagues do you trust, and for what?
<--- Score

34. Are all key stakeholders present at all Structured Walkthroughs?
<--- Score

35. What threat is Platform Positioning addressing?
<--- Score

36. How are you doing compared to your industry?
<--- Score

37. Do you have enough freaky customers in your portfolio pushing you to the limit day in and day out?
<--- Score

38. Instead of going to current contacts for new ideas, what if you reconnected with dormant contacts-- the people you used to know? If you were going reactivate a dormant tie, who would it be?
<--- Score

39. What would you recommend your friend do if he/she were facing this dilemma?
<--- Score

40. Who will be responsible for deciding whether Platform Positioning goes ahead or not after the initial investigations?
<--- Score

41. What happens when a new employee joins the organization?
<--- Score

42. Is there a work around that you can use?
<--- Score

43. What is the funding source for this project?
<--- Score

44. What is the kind of project structure that would be appropriate for your Platform Positioning project, should it be formal and complex, or can it be less formal and relatively simple?
<--- Score

45. What counts that you are not counting?
<--- Score

46. Who, on the executive team or the board, has spoken to a customer recently?
<--- Score

47. Which Platform Positioning goals are the most important?
<--- Score

48. Do you think you know, or do you know you know ?

<--- Score

49. How do you make it meaningful in connecting Platform Positioning with what users do day-to-day?

<--- Score

50. How do you assess the Platform Positioning pitfalls that are inherent in implementing it?

<--- Score

51. What are your personal philosophies regarding Platform Positioning and how do they influence your work?

<--- Score

52. Why should you adopt a Platform Positioning framework?

<--- Score

53. How do you deal with Platform Positioning changes?

<--- Score

54. Would you rather sell to knowledgeable and informed customers or to uninformed customers?

<--- Score

55. Do you see more potential in people than they do in themselves?

<--- Score

56. What are the long-term Platform Positioning goals?

<--- Score

57. If you got fired and a new hire took your place, what would she do different?
<--- Score

58. What are the gaps in your knowledge and experience?
<--- Score

59. If you do not follow, then how to lead?
<--- Score

60. Are your responses positive or negative?
<--- Score

61. Are you relevant? Will you be relevant five years from now? Ten?
<--- Score

62. What are the key enablers to make this Platform Positioning move?
<--- Score

63. How can you become the company that would put you out of business?
<--- Score

64. Ask yourself: how would you do this work if you only had one staff member to do it?
<--- Score

65. Who do you think the world wants your organization to be?
<--- Score

66. Can you break it down?

<--- Score

67. What are the rules and assumptions your industry operates under? What if the opposite were true?
<--- Score

68. Why is Platform Positioning important for you now?
<--- Score

69. How do you proactively clarify deliverables and Platform Positioning quality expectations?
<--- Score

70. If there were zero limitations, what would you do differently?
<--- Score

71. How do you lead with Platform Positioning in mind?
<--- Score

72. What projects are going on in the organization today, and what resources are those projects using from the resource pools?
<--- Score

73. What is the range of capabilities?
<--- Score

74. How can you incorporate support to ensure safe and effective use of Platform Positioning into the services that you provide?
<--- Score

75. Which individuals, teams or departments will be

involved in Platform Positioning?

<--- Score

76. Are you satisfied with your current role? If not, what is missing from it?

<--- Score

77. How will you ensure you get what you expected?

<--- Score

78. What is the estimated value of the project?

<--- Score

79. Do Platform Positioning rules make a reasonable demand on a users capabilities?

<--- Score

80. What does your signature ensure?

<--- Score

81. What have you done to protect your business from competitive encroachment?

<--- Score

82. What should you stop doing?

<--- Score

83. In the past year, what have you done (or could you have done) to increase the accurate perception of your company/brand as ethical and honest?

<--- Score

84. What is your Platform Positioning strategy?

<--- Score

85. What business benefits will Platform Positioning goals deliver if achieved?
<--- Score

86. If you had to rebuild your organization without any traditional competitive advantages (i.e., no killer technology, promising research, innovative product/service delivery model, etcetera), how would your people have to approach their work and collaborate together in order to create the necessary conditions for success?
<--- Score

87. How do you listen to customers to obtain actionable information?
<--- Score

88. Who are four people whose careers you have enhanced?
<--- Score

89. If you had to leave your organization for a year and the only communication you could have with employees/colleagues was a single paragraph, what would you write?
<--- Score

90. What are the challenges?
<--- Score

91. Can you maintain your growth without detracting from the factors that have contributed to your success?
<--- Score

92. Who is responsible for ensuring appropriate resources (time, people and money) are allocated to Platform Positioning?
<--- Score

93. How do you accomplish your long range Platform Positioning goals?
<--- Score

94. Is it economical; do you have the time and money?
<--- Score

95. What must you excel at?
<--- Score

96. Who are your customers?
<--- Score

97. Why do and why don't your customers like your organization?
<--- Score

98. Do you have an implicit bias for capital investments over people investments?
<--- Score

99. Is a Platform Positioning team work effort in place?
<--- Score

100. What did you miss in the interview for the worst hire you ever made?
<--- Score

101. Is a Platform Positioning breakthrough on the horizon?
<--- Score

102. What are the top 3 things at the forefront of your Platform Positioning agendas for the next 3 years?
<--- Score

103. How much contingency will be available in the budget?
<--- Score

104. What is the overall talent health of your organization as a whole at senior levels, and for each organization reporting to a member of the Senior Leadership Team?
<--- Score

105. What are the performance and scale of the Platform Positioning tools?
<--- Score

106. Has implementation been effective in reaching specified objectives so far?
<--- Score

107. How do you know if you are successful?
<--- Score

108. How do you engage the workforce, in addition to satisfying them?
<--- Score

109. Who will provide the final approval of Platform Positioning deliverables?
<--- Score

110. Who uses your product in ways you never expected?

<--- Score

111. How do you set Platform Positioning stretch targets and how do you get people to not only participate in setting these stretch targets but also that they strive to achieve these?
<--- Score

112. Who is responsible for errors?
<--- Score

113. Do you know what you are doing? And who do you call if you don't?
<--- Score

114. If you were responsible for initiating and implementing major changes in your organization, what steps might you take to ensure acceptance of those changes?
<--- Score

115. Political -is anyone trying to undermine this project?
<--- Score

116. What are strategies for increasing support and reducing opposition?
<--- Score

117. What are you challenging?
<--- Score

118. If your company went out of business tomorrow, would anyone who doesn't get a paycheck here care?
<--- Score

119. How do you manage Platform Positioning Knowledge Management (KM)?
<--- Score

120. How long will it take to change?
<--- Score

121. Why not do Platform Positioning?
<--- Score

122. Who have you, as a company, historically been when you've been at your best?
<--- Score

123. What is the purpose of Platform Positioning in relation to the mission?
<--- Score

124. What is something you believe that nearly no one agrees with you on?
<--- Score

125. Who is the main stakeholder, with ultimate responsibility for driving Platform Positioning forward?
<--- Score

126. What you are going to do to affect the numbers?
<--- Score

127. How do you foster the skills, knowledge, talents, attributes, and characteristics you want to have?
<--- Score

128. Who do you want your customers to become?
<--- Score

129. Who will determine interim and final deadlines?
<--- Score

130. What have been your experiences in defining long range Platform Positioning goals?
<--- Score

131. If you find that you havent accomplished one of the goals for one of the steps of the Platform Positioning strategy, what will you do to fix it?
<--- Score

132. What could happen if you do not do it?
<--- Score

133. What will be the consequences to the stakeholder (financial, reputation etc) if Platform Positioning does not go ahead or fails to deliver the objectives?
<--- Score

134. Are the assumptions believable and achievable?
<--- Score

135. If you weren't already in this business, would you enter it today? And if not, what are you going to do about it?
<--- Score

136. Do you have the right capabilities and capacities?
<--- Score

137. Can the schedule be done in the given time?
<--- Score

138. Do you have past Platform Positioning successes?
<--- Score

139. Why should people listen to you?
<--- Score

140. Are there any activities that you can take off your to do list?
<--- Score

141. How do you foster innovation?
<--- Score

142. Are you changing as fast as the world around you?
<--- Score

143. Is there any existing Platform Positioning governance structure?
<--- Score

144. What is your competitive advantage?
<--- Score

145. What one word do you want to own in the minds of your customers, employees, and partners?
<--- Score

146. At what moment would you think; Will I get fired?
<--- Score

147. How do senior leaders deploy your organizations vision and values through your leadership system, to

the workforce, to key suppliers and partners, and to customers and other stakeholders, as appropriate?
<--- Score

148. What are the usability implications of Platform Positioning actions?
<--- Score

149. How do you provide a safe environment -physically and emotionally?
<--- Score

150. Which models, tools and techniques are necessary?
<--- Score

151. How much does Platform Positioning help?
<--- Score

152. How do you maintain Platform Positioning's Integrity?
<--- Score

153. What are the success criteria that will indicate that Platform Positioning objectives have been met and the benefits delivered?
<--- Score

154. How will you know that the Platform Positioning project has been successful?
<--- Score

155. What is effective Platform Positioning?
<--- Score

156. How likely is it that a customer would

recommend your company to a friend or colleague?
<--- Score

157. How do you govern and fulfill your societal responsibilities?
<--- Score

158. Why will customers want to buy your organizations products/services?
<--- Score

159. Operational - will it work?
<--- Score

160. Is there any reason to believe the opposite of my current belief?
<--- Score

161. Who are the key stakeholders?
<--- Score

162. What new services of functionality will be implemented next with Platform Positioning ?
<--- Score

163. Who is responsible for Platform Positioning?
<--- Score

164. Did your employees make progress today?
<--- Score

165. How can you become more high-tech but still be high touch?
<--- Score

166. What is your formula for success in Platform

Positioning ?

<--- Score

167. Do you have the right people on the bus?

<--- Score

168. Is Platform Positioning dependent on the successful delivery of a current project?

<--- Score

169. Why is it important to have senior management support for a Platform Positioning project?

<--- Score

170. How do you go about securing Platform Positioning?

<--- Score

171. If no one would ever find out about your accomplishments, how would you lead differently?

<--- Score

172. Is your basic point _____ or _____?

<--- Score

173. What trophy do you want on your mantle?

<--- Score

174. Do you say no to customers for no reason?

<--- Score

175. What is a feasible sequencing of reform initiatives over time?

<--- Score

176. Can you do all this work?

<--- Score

177. What is your BATNA (best alternative to a negotiated agreement)?
<--- Score

178. How do you track customer value, profitability or financial return, organizational success, and sustainability?
<--- Score

179. What are the potential basics of Platform Positioning fraud?
<--- Score

180. What goals did you miss?
<--- Score

181. What Platform Positioning skills are most important?
<--- Score

182. Is maximizing Platform Positioning protection the same as minimizing Platform Positioning loss?
<--- Score

183. What information is critical to your organization that your executives are ignoring?
<--- Score

184. What is the big Platform Positioning idea?
<--- Score

185. Are assumptions made in Platform Positioning stated explicitly?
<--- Score

186. Are the criteria for selecting recommendations stated?
<--- Score

187. Which functions and people interact with the supplier and or customer?
<--- Score

188. What is it like to work for you?
<--- Score

189. How do customers see your organization?
<--- Score

190. What are the short and long-term Platform Positioning goals?
<--- Score

191. How do you keep the momentum going?
<--- Score

192. Marketing budgets are tighter, consumers are more skeptical, and social media has changed forever the way we talk about Platform Positioning, how do you gain traction?
<--- Score

193. What are the business goals Platform Positioning is aiming to achieve?
<--- Score

194. What is the recommended frequency of auditing?
<--- Score

195. What are internal and external Platform

Positioning relations?
<--- Score

196. What may be the consequences for the performance of an organization if all stakeholders are not consulted regarding Platform Positioning?
<--- Score

197. Will there be any necessary staff changes (redundancies or new hires)?
<--- Score

198. Will it be accepted by users?
<--- Score

199. How do you create buy-in?
<--- Score

Add up total points for this section:
_____ = Total points for this section

Divided by: _____ (number of statements answered) = _____
Average score for this section

Transfer your score to the Platform Positioning Index at the beginning of the Self-Assessment.

Platform Positioning and Managing Projects, Criteria for Project Managers:

1.0 Initiating Process Group: Platform Positioning

1. During which stage of Risk planning are modeling techniques used to determine overall effects of risks on Platform Positioning project objectives for high probability, high impact risks?

2. Have you evaluated the teams performance and asked for feedback?

3. What is the NEXT thing to do?

4. What are the pressing issues of the hour?

5. Are you certain deliverables are properly completed and meet quality standards?

6. Just how important is your work to the overall success of the Platform Positioning project?

7. How is each deliverable reviewed, verified, and validated?

8. What were the challenges that you encountered during the execution of a previous Platform Positioning project that you would not want to repeat?

9. Do you know all the stakeholders impacted by the Platform Positioning project and what needs are?

10. Who supports, improves, and oversees standardized processes related to the Platform Positioning projects program?

11. At which stage, in a typical Platform Positioning project do stake holders have maximum influence?

12. What are the inputs required to produce the deliverables?

13. At which cmmi level are software processes documented, standardized, and integrated into a standard to-be practiced process for your organization?

14. Who is performing the work of the Platform Positioning project?

15. During which stage of Risk planning are risks prioritized based on probability and impact?

16. When must it be done?

17. Which six sigma dmaic phase focuses on why and how defects and errors occur?

18. Establishment of pm office?

19. Are you just doing busywork to pass the time?

20. Did the Platform Positioning project team have the right skills?

1.1 Project Charter: Platform Positioning

21. Avoid costs, improve service, and/ or comply with a mandate?

22. Strategic fit: what is the strategic initiative identifier for this Platform Positioning project?

23. How do you manage integration?

24. Environmental stewardship and sustainability considerations: what is the process that will be used to ensure compliance with the environmental stewardship policy?

25. Who are the stakeholders?

26. Where and how does the team fit within your organization structure?

27. What is the most common tool for helping define the detail?

28. How much?

29. If finished, on what date did it finish?

30. What are the assigned resources?

31. Assumptions and constraints: what assumptions were made in defining the Platform Positioning project?

32. Is time of the essence?

33. Are you building in-house ?

34. For whom?

35. Platform Positioning project background: what is the primary motivation for this Platform Positioning project?

36. Why do you manage integration?

37. How will you know that a change is an improvement?

38. Must Have?

39. Platform Positioning project objective statement: what must the Platform Positioning project do?

40. Who manages integration?

1.2 Stakeholder Register: Platform Positioning

41. Who is managing stakeholder engagement?

42. How will reports be created?

43. Who wants to talk about Security?

44. What & Why?

45. How big is the gap?

46. What is the power of the stakeholder?

47. Is your organization ready for change?

48. How much influence do they have on the Platform Positioning project?

49. How should employers make voices heard?

50. What opportunities exist to provide communications?

51. What are the major Platform Positioning project milestones requiring communications or providing communications opportunities?

1.3 Stakeholder Analysis Matrix: Platform Positioning

52. What is the issue at stake?

53. What should thwe organizations stakeholders avoid?

54. What organizational arrangements are planned to ensure the Platform Positioning project achieves its social development outcomes?

55. What can the Platform Positioning projects outcome be used for?

56. What are the mechanisms of public and social accountability, and how can they be made better?

57. How can you fill the need to show progress?

58. Innovative aspects?

59. Reliability of data, plan predictability?

60. Are you going to weigh the stakeholders?

61. Does your organization have bad debt or cash-flow problems?

62. Insurmountable weaknesses?

63. Volumes, production, economies?

64. What are the opportunities for communication?

65. How to measure the achievement of the Development Objective?

66. Is there a reason why you are or are not not using an external rating system?

67. What resources might the stakeholder bring to the Platform Positioning project?

68. Are there different rules or organizational models for men and women?

69. Environmental effects?

70. Business and product development?

71. What is in it for you?

2.0 Planning Process Group: Platform Positioning

72. First of all, should any action be taken?

73. How will you do it?

74. How many days can task X be late in starting without affecting the Platform Positioning project completion date?

75. To what extent is the program helping to influence your organizations policy framework?

76. In what ways can the governance of the Platform Positioning project be improved so that it has greater likelihood of achieving future sustainability?

77. How can you make your needs known?

78. Does it make any difference if you are successful?

79. To what extent has a PMO contributed to raising the quality of the design of the Platform Positioning project?

80. What is the critical path for this Platform Positioning project, and what is the duration of the critical path?

81. Is the duration of the program sufficient to ensure a cycle that will Platform Positioning project the sustainability of the interventions?

82. How well defined and documented are the Platform Positioning project management processes you chose to use?

83. When will the Platform Positioning project be done?

84. What factors are contributing to progress or delay in the achievement of products and results?

85. What makes your Platform Positioning project successful?

86. Explanation: is what the Platform Positioning project intents to solve a hard question?

87. In which Platform Positioning project management process group is the detailed Platform Positioning project budget created?

88. Did the program design/ implementation strategy adequately address the planning stage necessary to set up structures, hire staff etc.?

89. On which process should team members spend the most time?

90. To what extent have the target population and participants made the activities own, taking an active role in it?

2.1 Project Management Plan: Platform Positioning

91. Are there any Client staffing expectations?

92. How do you organize the costs in the Platform Positioning project management plan?

93. What is the justification?

94. Does the implementation plan have an appropriate division of responsibilities?

95. What happened during the process that you found interesting?

96. Is mitigation authorized or recommended?

97. What are the deliverables?

98. What worked well?

99. Are there non-structural buyout or relocation recommendations?

100. What did not work so well?

101. Is there anything you would now do differently on your Platform Positioning project based on past experience?

102. Who is the Platform Positioning project Manager?

103. What would you do differently what did not work?

104. Are there any windfall benefits that would accrue to the Platform Positioning project sponsor or other parties?

105. What goes into your Platform Positioning project Charter?

106. Will you add a schedule and diagram?

107. Is the engineering content at a feasibility level-of-detail, and is it sufficiently complete, to provide an adequate basis for the baseline cost estimate?

108. Is there an incremental analysis/cost effectiveness analysis of proposed mitigation features based on an approved method and using an accepted model?

109. Are cost risk analysis methods applied to develop contingencies for the estimated total Platform Positioning project costs?

110. Is the budget realistic?

2.2 Scope Management Plan: Platform Positioning

111. Have the personnel with the necessary skills and competence been identified and has agreement for participation in the Platform Positioning project been reached with the appropriate management?

112. Have all involved Platform Positioning project stakeholders and work groups committed to the Platform Positioning project?

113. Is there a formal process for updating the Platform Positioning project baseline?

114. Function of the configuration control board?

115. Are vendor contract reports, reviews and visits conducted periodically?

116. Are the proposed Platform Positioning project purposes different than the previously authorized Platform Positioning project?

117. Are adequate resources provided for the quality assurance function?

118. How relevant is this attribute to this Platform Positioning project or audit?

119. Has stakeholder analysis been conducted, assessing influence on the Platform Positioning project and authority levels?

120. Is it standard practice to formally commit stakeholders to the Platform Positioning project via agreements?

121. Is there an on-going process in place to monitor Platform Positioning project risks?

122. Are internal Platform Positioning project status meetings held at reasonable intervals?

123. What is the unique product, service or result?

124. What is the need the Platform Positioning project will address?

125. Has a provision been made to reassess Platform Positioning project risks at various Platform Positioning project stages?

126. Do you have funding for Platform Positioning project and product development, implementation and on-going support?

127. How do you know how you are doing?

128. Is there a formal set of procedures supporting Issues Management?

129. Did your Platform Positioning project ask for this?

2.3 Requirements Management Plan: Platform Positioning

130. Is infrastructure setup part of your Platform Positioning project?

131. Do you have an appropriate arrangement for meetings?

132. If it exists, where is it housed?

133. Is the change control process documented?

134. Which hardware or software, related to, or as outcome of the Platform Positioning project is new to your organization?

135. How will requirements be managed?

136. Business analysis scope?

137. Who will finally present the work or product(s) for acceptance?

138. Should you include sub-activities?

139. Is the system software (non-operating system) new to the IT Platform Positioning project team?

140. Are actual resource expenditures versus planned still acceptable?

141. Do you really need to write this document at all?

142. Have stakeholders been instructed in the Change Control process?

143. Controlling Platform Positioning project requirements involves monitoring the status of the Platform Positioning project requirements and managing changes to the requirements. Who is responsible for monitoring and tracking the Platform Positioning project requirements?

144. Is it new or replacing an existing business system or process?

145. Did you provide clear and concise specifications?

146. Did you get proper approvals?

147. What performance metrics will be used?

148. What are you trying to do?

149. Describe the process for rejecting the Platform Positioning project requirements. Who has the authority to reject Platform Positioning project requirements?

2.4 Requirements Documentation: Platform Positioning

150. Where do you define what is a customer, what are the attributes of customer?

151. The problem with gathering requirements is right there in the word gathering. What images does it conjure?

152. What is the risk associated with the technology?

153. Are there legal issues?

154. Who is interacting with the system?

155. What if the system wasn t implemented?

156. Does your organization restrict technical alternatives?

157. How does the proposed Platform Positioning project contribute to the overall objectives of your organization?

158. Consistency. are there any requirements conflicts?

159. How will requirements be documented and who signs off on them?

160. Basic work/business process; high-level, what is being touched?

161. What is a show stopper in the requirements?

162. Verifiability. can the requirements be checked?

163. What is effective documentation?

164. How much does requirements engineering cost?

165. Do your constraints stand?

166. How does what is being described meet the business need?

167. What is your Elevator Speech?

168. Completeness. are all functions required by the customer included?

169. Can the requirement be changed without a large impact on other requirements?

2.5 Requirements Traceability Matrix: Platform Positioning

170. What is the WBS?

171. How will it affect the stakeholders personally in career?

172. Why do you manage scope?

173. What percentage of Platform Positioning projects are producing traceability matrices between requirements and other work products?

174. How small is small enough?

175. Why use a WBS?

176. Is there a requirements traceability process in place?

177. Will you use a Requirements Traceability Matrix?

178. How do you manage scope?

179. Describe the process for approving requirements so they can be added to the traceability matrix and Platform Positioning project work can be performed. Will the Platform Positioning project requirements become approved in writing?

180. Do you have a clear understanding of all subcontracts in place?

181. What are the chronologies, contingencies, consequences, criteria?

2.6 Project Scope Statement: Platform Positioning

182. Elements of scope management that deal with concept development ?

183. How often do you estimate that the scope might change, and why?

184. Is your organization structure appropriate for the Platform Positioning projects size and complexity?

185. How often will scope changes be reviewed?

186. What went right?

187. Is the plan for your organization of the Platform Positioning project resources adequate?

188. Elements that deal with providing the detail?

189. If the scope changes, what will the impact be to your Platform Positioning project in terms of duration, cost, quality, or any other important areas of the Platform Positioning project?

190. Will the qa related information be reported regularly as part of the status reporting mechanisms?

191. Does the scope statement still need some clarity?

192. Will there be a Change Control Process in place?

193. Risks?

194. How will you verify the accuracy of the work of the Platform Positioning project, and what constitutes acceptance of the deliverables?

195. Will the risk documents be filed?

196. Will all tasks resulting from issues be entered into the Platform Positioning project Plan and tracked through the plan?

197. Have you been able to easily identify success criteria and create objective measurements for each of the Platform Positioning project scopes goal statements?

198. Relevant - ask yourself can you get there; why are you doing this Platform Positioning project?

199. Is the Platform Positioning project sponsor function identified and defined?

2.7 Assumption and Constraint Log: Platform Positioning

200. How are new requirements or changes to requirements identified?

201. Were the system requirements formally reviewed prior to initiating the design phase?

202. Do you know what your customers expectations are regarding this process?

203. Are there processes defining how software will be developed including development methods, overall timeline for development, software product standards, and traceability?

204. Are formal code reviews conducted?

205. Do documented requirements exist for all critical components and areas, including technical, business, interfaces, performance, security and conversion requirements?

206. Is the process working, and people are not executing in compliance of the process?

207. Are processes for release management of new development from coding and unit testing, to integration testing, to training, and production defined and followed?

208. Have adequate resources been provided by

management to ensure Platform Positioning project success?

209. Model-building: what data-analytic strategies are useful when building proportional-hazards models?

210. How can you prevent/fix violations?

211. Does a specific action and/or state that is known to violate security policy occur?

212. Have all stakeholders been identified?

213. Are there unnecessary steps that are creating bottlenecks and/or causing people to wait?

214. After observing execution of process, is it in compliance with the documented Plan?

215. Is staff trained on the software technologies that are being used on the Platform Positioning project?

216. What to do at recovery?

217. Is the steering committee active in Platform Positioning project oversight?

218. Are funding and staffing resource estimates sufficiently detailed and documented for use in planning and tracking the Platform Positioning project?

219. Are requirements management tracking tools and procedures in place?

2.8 Work Breakdown Structure: Platform Positioning

220. When does it have to be done?

221. Do you need another level?

222. Who has to do it?

223. What is the probability of completing the Platform Positioning project in less that xx days?

224. Can you make it?

225. Is the work breakdown structure (wbs) defined and is the scope of the Platform Positioning project clear with assigned deliverable owners?

226. When would you develop a Work Breakdown Structure?

227. Why is it useful?

228. When do you stop?

229. Is it still viable?

230. How many levels?

231. Where does it take place?

232. Why would you develop a Work Breakdown Structure?

233. How big is a work-package?

234. How much detail?

235. How far down?

2.9 WBS Dictionary: Platform Positioning

236. The anticipated business volume?

237. Budgets assigned to major functional organizations?

238. Are the wbs and organizational levels for application of the Platform Positioning projected overhead costs identified?

239. Are the bases and rates for allocating costs from each indirect pool to commercial work consistent with the already stated used to allocate corresponding costs to Government contracts?

240. Does the cost accumulation system provide for summarization of indirect costs from the point of allocation to the contract total?

241. Are work packages reasonably short in time duration or do they have adequate objective indicators/milestones to minimize subjectivity of the in process work evaluation?

242. Are the rates for allocating costs from each indirect cost pool to contracts updated as necessary to ensure a realistic monthly allocation of indirect costs without significant year-end adjustments?

243. Authorization to proceed with all authorized work?

244. Major functional areas of contract effort?

245. What is the end result of a work package?

246. Does the contractor have procedures which permit identification of recurring or non-recurring costs as necessary?

247. Is work properly classified as measured effort, LOE, or apportioned effort and appropriately separated?

248. Are indirect costs charged to the appropriate indirect pools and incurring organization?

249. Is future work which cannot be planned in detail subdivided to the extent practicable for budgeting and scheduling purposes?

250. Are estimates of costs at completion utilized in determining contract funding requirements and reporting them?

251. Budgeted cost for work performed?

252. Are records maintained to show how management reserves are used?

253. Are there procedures for monitoring action items and corrective actions to the point of resolution and are corresponding procedures being followed?

254. Does the contractors system provide for determination of price variance by comparing planned Vs actual commitments?

2.10 Schedule Management Plan: Platform Positioning

255. Personnel with expertise?

256. Is funded schedule margin reasonable and logically distributed?

257. Has a quality assurance plan been developed for the Platform Positioning project?

258. Are written status reports provided on a designated frequent basis?

259. Are risk triggers captured?

260. Is the communication plan being followed?

261. Does the schedule have reasonable float?

262. Perform reality checks on schedules – are all tasks included?

263. Are post milestone Platform Positioning project reviews (PMPR) conducted with your organization at least once a year?

264. What happens if a warning is triggered?

265. What strengths do you have?

266. Is the steering committee active in Platform Positioning project oversight?

267. Is a process defined for baseline approval and control?

268. Are the payment terms being followed?

269. Are corrective actions and variances reported?

270. Are Platform Positioning project leaders committed to this Platform Positioning project full time?

271. Is there an excessive and invalid use of task constraints and relationships of leads/lags?

272. Is the critical path valid?

273. Will rolling way planning be used?

2.11 Activity List: Platform Positioning

274. How do you determine the late start (LS) for each activity?

275. What will be performed?

276. When do the individual activities need to start and finish?

277. What went well?

278. How should ongoing costs be monitored to try to keep the Platform Positioning project within budget?

279. What are you counting on?

280. How detailed should a Platform Positioning project get?

281. In what sequence?

282. How difficult will it be to do specific activities on this Platform Positioning project?

283. Is infrastructure setup part of your Platform Positioning project?

284. Where will it be performed?

285. How will it be performed?

286. For other activities, how much delay can be tolerated?

287. What did not go as well?

288. Who will perform the work?

289. Are the required resources available or need to be acquired?

290. What is your organizations history in doing similar activities?

291. What is the probability the Platform Positioning project can be completed in xx weeks?

2.12 Activity Attributes: Platform Positioning

292. Is there a trend during the year?

293. How many resources do you need to complete the work scope within a limit of X number of days?

294. Activity: fair or not fair?

295. Does your organization of the data change its meaning?

296. Have you identified the Activity Leveling Priority code value on each activity?

297. How much activity detail is required?

298. Can more resources be added?

299. Have constraints been applied to the start and finish milestones for the phases?

300. Resource is assigned to?

301. Activity: what is In the Bag?

302. Activity: what is Missing?

303. Were there other ways you could have organized the data to achieve similar results?

304. Are the required resources available?

305. Would you consider either of corresponding activities an outlier?

306. Which method produces the more accurate cost assignment?

307. Can you re-assign any activities to another resource to resolve an over-allocation?

308. How difficult will it be to do specific activities on this Platform Positioning project?

309. What is missing?

2.13 Milestone List: Platform Positioning

310. What has been done so far?

311. Loss of key staff?

312. What specific improvements did you make to the Platform Positioning project proposal since the previous time?

313. What background experience, skills, and strengths does the team bring to your organization?

314. What is the market for your technology, product or service?

315. Effects on core activities, distraction?

316. Timescales, deadlines and pressures?

317. Political effects?

318. Which path is the critical path?

319. Identify critical paths (one or more) and which activities are on the critical path?

320. Sustaining internal capabilities?

321. Describe the concept of the technology, product or service that will be or has been developed. How will it be used?

322. How late can each activity be finished and started?

323. How will the milestone be verified?

324. Do you foresee any technical risks or developmental challenges?

325. Sustainable financial backing?

2.14 Network Diagram: Platform Positioning

326. What job or jobs could run concurrently?

327. What activities must occur simultaneously with this activity?

328. Will crashing x weeks return more in benefits than it costs?

329. What activity must be completed immediately before this activity can start?

330. How difficult will it be to do specific activities on this Platform Positioning project?

331. What is the probability of completing the Platform Positioning project in less that xx days?

332. What must be completed before an activity can be started?

333. What is the completion time?

334. If x is long, what would be the completion time if you break x into two parallel parts of y weeks and z weeks?

335. Can you calculate the confidence level?

336. What are the Major Administrative Issues?

337. Why must you schedule milestones, such as reviews, throughout the Platform Positioning project?

338. What job or jobs follow it?

339. Review the logical flow of the network diagram. Take a look at which activities you have first and then sequence the activities. Do they make sense?

340. If the Platform Positioning project network diagram cannot change and you have extra personnel resources, what is the BEST thing to do?

341. If a current contract exists, can you provide the vendor name, contract start, and contract expiration date?

342. What to do and When?

343. Where do schedules come from?

344. Where do you schedule uncertainty time?

2.15 Activity Resource Requirements: Platform Positioning

345. How do you handle petty cash?

346. Why do you do that?

347. When does monitoring begin?

348. Which logical relationship does the PDM use most often?

349. How many signatures do you require on a check and does this match what is in your policy and procedures?

350. Time for overtime?

351. Are there unresolved issues that need to be addressed?

352. Is there anything planned that does not need to be here?

353. What is the Work Plan Standard?

354. Do you use tools like decomposition and rolling-wave planning to produce the activity list and other outputs?

355. Anything else?

356. Organizational Applicability?

357. Other support in specific areas?

358. How do you manage time?

359. What are constraints that you might find during the Human Resource Planning process?

2.16 Resource Breakdown Structure: Platform Positioning

360. Who needs what information?

361. Why do you do it?

362. What defines a successful Platform Positioning project?

363. What are the requirements for resource data?

364. What is the purpose of assigning and documenting responsibility?

365. Why time management?

366. What is Platform Positioning project communication management?

367. How difficult will it be to do specific activities on this Platform Positioning project?

368. What is the primary purpose of the human resource plan?

369. What is the difference between % Complete and % work?

370. Who delivers the information?

371. What defines a successful Platform Positioning project?

372. Who will use the system?

373. Who will be used as a Platform Positioning project team member?

374. Which resources should be in the resource pool?

375. How should the information be delivered?

376. Changes based on input from stakeholders?

2.17 Activity Duration Estimates: Platform Positioning

377. What are the largest companies that provide information technology outsourcing services?

378. Are inspections completed to determine if the results comply with the requirements?

379. Consider the common sources of risk on information technology Platform Positioning projects and suggestions for managing them. Which suggestions do you find most useful?

380. Are steps identified by which Platform Positioning project documents may be changed?

381. What are the nine areas of expertise?

382. Which includes asking team members about the time estimates for activities and reaching agreement on the calendar date for each activity?

383. Does a process exist to identify individuals authorized to make certain decisions?

384. What is the shortest possible time it will take to complete this Platform Positioning project?

385. Does a process exist to determine which risk events to accept and which events to disregard?

386. Does the case present a realistic scenario?

387. What tasks must precede this task?

388. Do they make sense?

389. It under budget or over budget?

390. What is the BEST thing for the Platform Positioning project manager to do?

391. Are processes defined to monitor Platform Positioning project cost and schedule variances?

392. Do Platform Positioning project team members work in the same physical location to enhance team performance?

393. When a risk event occurs, is the risk response evaluated and the appropriate response implemented?

394. Briefly summarize the work done by Maslow, Herzberg, McClellan, McGregor, Ouchi, Thamhain and Wilemon, and Covey. How do theories relate to Platform Positioning project management?

395. What are the typical challenges Platform Positioning project teams face during each of the five process groups?

396. Who will provide training for the new application?

2.18 Duration Estimating Worksheet: Platform Positioning

397. Why estimate costs?

398. What questions do you have?

399. Why estimate time and cost?

400. What utility impacts are there?

401. How can the Platform Positioning project be displayed graphically to better visualize the activities?

402. What is cost and Platform Positioning project cost management?

403. What is an Average Platform Positioning project?

404. Done before proceeding with this activity or what can be done concurrently?

405. Do any colleagues have experience with your organization and/or RFPs?

406. Does the Platform Positioning project provide innovative ways for stakeholders to overcome obstacles or deliver better outcomes?

407. Will the Platform Positioning project collaborate with the local community and leverage resources?

408. What is your role?

409. What is next?

410. What went wrong?

411. When does your organization expect to be able to complete it?

412. Is the Platform Positioning project responsive to community need?

413. What is the total time required to complete the Platform Positioning project if no delays occur?

414. How should ongoing costs be monitored to try to keep the Platform Positioning project within budget?

2.19 Project Schedule: Platform Positioning

415. How much slack is available in the Platform Positioning project?

416. If you can not fix it, how do you do it differently?

417. How closely did the initial Platform Positioning project Schedule compare with the actual schedule?

418. Is the Platform Positioning project schedule available for all Platform Positioning project team members to review?

419. Verify that the update is accurate. Are all remaining durations correct?

420. Does the condition or event threaten the Platform Positioning projects objectives in any ways?

421. Are the original Platform Positioning project schedule and budget realistic?

422. How detailed should a Platform Positioning project get?

423. How do you manage Platform Positioning project Risk?

424. Why do you think schedule issues often cause the most conflicts on Platform Positioning projects?

425. Did the Platform Positioning project come in under budget?

426. Why is software Platform Positioning project disaster so common?

427. Are key risk mitigation strategies added to the Platform Positioning project schedule?

428. To what degree is do you feel the entire team was committed to the Platform Positioning project schedule?

429. Is Platform Positioning project work proceeding in accordance with the original Platform Positioning project schedule?

430. How does a Platform Positioning project get to be a year late ?

431. What is risk management?

2.20 Cost Management Plan: Platform Positioning

432. Is documentation created for communication with the suppliers and Vendors?

433. Are issues raised, assessed, actioned, and resolved in a timely and efficient manner?

434. What is the work breakdown structure for the Platform Positioning project?

435. Is the Platform Positioning project schedule available for all Platform Positioning project team members to review?

436. Contracting method – what contracting method is to be used for the contracts?

437. Is Platform Positioning project status reviewed with the steering and executive teams at appropriate intervals?

438. Risk Analysis?

439. Are non-critical path items updated and agreed upon with the teams?

440. Are schedule deliverables actually delivered?

441. Are the appropriate IT resources adequate to meet planned commitments?

442. Has the scope management document been updated and distributed to help prevent scope creep?

443. Are Platform Positioning project leaders committed to this Platform Positioning project full time?

444. Contingency – how will cost contingency be administered?

445. Are all resource assumptions documented?

446. Why do you manage cost?

447. Has your organization readiness assessment been conducted?

448. Are Platform Positioning project team members involved in detailed estimating and scheduling?

449. Is there an onboarding process in place?

450. Risk rating?

451. Cost tracking and performance analysis – How will cost tracking and performance analysis be accomplished?

2.21 Activity Cost Estimates: Platform Positioning

452. What are the audit requirements?

453. Does the estimator estimate by task or by person?

454. Who determines the quality and expertise of contractors?

455. Was the consultant knowledgeable about the program?

456. How do you change activities?

457. Eac -estimate at completion, what is the total job expected to cost?

458. Maintenance Reserve?

459. Were the costs or charges reasonable?

460. Are data needed on characteristics of care?

461. Review – what are some common errors in activities to avoid?

462. What makes a good expected result statement?

463. What defines a successful Platform Positioning project?

464. How and when do you enter into Platform Positioning project Procurement Management?

465. Can you change your activities?

466. How do you fund change orders?

467. Were escalated issues resolved promptly?

468. Where can you get activity reports?

469. What is the activity inventory?

2.22 Cost Estimating Worksheet: Platform Positioning

470. What costs are to be estimated?

471. What info is needed?

472. What will others want?

473. What happens to any remaining funds not used?

474. What is the estimated labor cost today based upon this information?

475. How will the results be shared and to whom?

476. Is it feasible to establish a control group arrangement?

477. Is the Platform Positioning project responsive to community need?

478. What can be included?

479. What is the purpose of estimating?

480. Will the Platform Positioning project collaborate with the local community and leverage resources?

481. Value pocket identification & quantification what are value pockets?

482. Who is best positioned to know and assist in

identifying corresponding factors?

483. What additional Platform Positioning project(s) could be initiated as a result of this Platform Positioning project?

484. Does the Platform Positioning project provide innovative ways for stakeholders to overcome obstacles or deliver better outcomes?

485. Identify the timeframe necessary to monitor progress and collect data to determine how the selected measure has changed?

486. Ask: are others positioned to know, are others credible, and will others cooperate?

487. Can a trend be established from historical performance data on the selected measure and are the criteria for using trend analysis or forecasting methods met?

2.23 Cost Baseline: Platform Positioning

488. Is there anything you need from upper management in order to be successful?

489. Is request in line with priorities?

490. Have all the product or service deliverables been accepted by the customer?

491. Has the Platform Positioning project (or Platform Positioning project phase) been evaluated against each objective established in the product description and Integrated Platform Positioning project Plan?

492. Where do changes come from?

493. What is it ?

494. Verify business objectives. Are others appropriate, and well-articulated?

495. Has the Platform Positioning projected annual cost to operate and maintain the product(s) or service(s) been approved and funded?

496. Have you identified skills that are missing from your team?

497. Impact to environment?

498. What threats might prevent you from getting

there?

499. Has the documentation relating to operation and maintenance of the product(s) or service(s) been delivered to, and accepted by, operations management?

500. On budget?

501. Has the Platform Positioning project documentation been archived or otherwise disposed as described in the Platform Positioning project communication plan?

502. Have the lessons learned been filed with the Platform Positioning project Management Office?

503. Have the resources used by the Platform Positioning project been reassigned to other units or Platform Positioning projects?

504. Has the actual cost of the Platform Positioning project (or Platform Positioning project phase) been tallied and compared to the approved budget?

505. How likely is it to go wrong?

506. Review your risk triggers -have your risks changed?

2.24 Quality Management Plan: Platform Positioning

507. Are decisions/actions based on data collected?

508. Are qmps good forever?

509. What field records are generated?

510. Contradictory information between document sections?

511. What are the established criteria that sampling / testing data are compared against?

512. What are your organizations key processes (product, service, business, and support)?

513. What process do you use to minimize errors, defects, and rework?

514. What are the appropriate test methods to be used?

515. With the five whys method, the team considers why the issue being explored occurred. do others then take that initial answer and ask why?

516. Documented results available?

517. What are you trying to accomplish?

518. Does the program use other agents to collect

samples?

519. Are there nonconformance issues?

520. What type of in-house testing do you conduct?

521. Is there a Quality Management Plan?

522. Are there procedures in place to effectively manage interdependencies with other Platform Positioning projects / systems?

523. What is quality and how will you ensure it?

524. Is staff trained on the software technologies that are being used on the Platform Positioning project?

2.25 Quality Metrics: Platform Positioning

525. Is quality culture a competitive advantage?

526. How do you calculate corresponding metrics?

527. What can manufacturing professionals do to ensure quality is seen as an integral part of the entire product lifecycle?

528. Subjective quality component: customer satisfaction, how do you measure it?

529. What is the timeline to meet your goal?

530. What does this tell us?

531. Are quality metrics defined?

532. How exactly do you define when differences exist?

533. What metrics do you measure?

534. When is the security analysis testing complete?

535. What happens if you get an abnormal result?

536. Did the team meet the Platform Positioning project success criteria documented in the Quality Metrics Matrix?

537. Were number of defects identified?

538. What metrics are important and most beneficial to measure?

539. What if the biggest risk to your business were the already stated people who do not complain?

540. How does one achieve stability?

541. Has it met internal or external standards?

542. What about still open problems?

543. How do you communicate results and findings to upper management?

544. What do you measure?

2.26 Process Improvement Plan: Platform Positioning

545. Who should prepare the process improvement action plan?

546. Have storage and access mechanisms and procedures been determined?

547. Are you making progress on the improvement framework?

548. Everyone agrees on what process improvement is, right?

549. Where do you want to be?

550. Does explicit definition of the measures exist?

551. To elicit goal statements, do you ask a question such as, What do you want to achieve?

552. Where are you now?

553. What lessons have you learned so far?

554. Have the supporting tools been developed or acquired?

555. Does your process ensure quality?

556. Are you making progress on your improvement plan?

557. What actions are needed to address the problems and achieve the goals?

558. Management commitment at all levels?

559. Are there forms and procedures to collect and record the data?

560. What is the return on investment?

561. Are you making progress on the goals?

562. Are you meeting the quality standards?

563. How do you manage quality?

2.27 Responsibility Assignment Matrix: Platform Positioning

564. Do managers and team members provide helpful suggestions during review meetings?

565. Changes in the nature of the overhead requirements?

566. The already stated responsible for overhead performance control of related costs?

567. Is work progressively subdivided into detailed work packages as requirements are defined?

568. Are all authorized tasks assigned to identified organizational elements?

569. Where does all this information come from?

570. Are authorized changes being incorporated in a timely manner?

571. Do you know how your people are allocated?

572. Are your organizations and items of cost assigned to each pool identified?

573. How cost benefit analysis?

574. What is the number one predictor of a groups productivity?

575. What are some important Platform Positioning project communications management tools?

576. What cost control tool do many experts say is crucial to Platform Positioning project management?

577. Are material costs reported within the same period as that in which BCWP is earned for that material?

578. What tool can show you individual and group allocations?

579. Performance to date and material commitment?

580. Do others have the time to dedicate to your Platform Positioning project?

581. Are meaningful indicators identified for use in measuring the status of cost and schedule performance?

582. Who is the sponsor?

2.28 Roles and Responsibilities: Platform Positioning

583. Who is responsible for implementation activities and where will the functions, roles and responsibilities be defined?

584. What should you do now to prepare for your career 5+ years from now?

585. Once the responsibilities are defined for the Platform Positioning project, have the deliverables, roles and responsibilities been clearly communicated to every participant?

586. Do you take the time to clearly define roles and responsibilities on Platform Positioning project tasks?

587. What is working well?

588. Is feedback clearly communicated and non-judgmental?

589. Are governance roles and responsibilities documented?

590. What are your major roles and responsibilities in the area of performance measurement and assessment?

591. Are Platform Positioning project team roles and responsibilities identified and documented?

592. What specific behaviors did you observe?

593. What expectations were met?

594. Do the values and practices inherent in the culture of your organization foster or hinder the process?

595. What expectations were NOT met?

596. Influence: what areas of organizational decision making are you able to influence when you do not have authority to make the final decision?

597. Key conclusions and recommendations: Are conclusions and recommendations relevant and acceptable?

598. Was the expectation clearly communicated?

599. Are the quality assurance functions and related roles and responsibilities clearly defined?

600. Concern: where are you limited or have no authority, where you can not influence?

601. Implementation of actions: Who are the responsible units?

2.29 Human Resource Management Plan: Platform Positioning

602. Has a sponsor been identified?

603. Is there a formal set of procedures supporting Stakeholder Management?

604. Have process improvement efforts been completed before requirements efforts begin?

605. Based on your Platform Positioning project communication management plan, what worked well?

606. Were the budget estimates reasonable?

607. Has the Platform Positioning project scope been baselined?

608. Have all involved Platform Positioning project stakeholders and work groups committed to the Platform Positioning project?

609. Are decisions captured in a decisions log?

610. Have all necessary approvals been obtained?

611. Does a documented Platform Positioning project organizational policy & plan (i.e. governance model) exist?

612. Is this Platform Positioning project carried out in

partnership with other groups/organizations?

613. Platform Positioning project Objectives?

614. Are staff skills known and available for each task?

615. Has a structured approach been used to break work effort into manageable components (WBS)?

616. Have reserves been created to address risks?

617. What were things that you need to improve?

618. Are updated Platform Positioning project time & resource estimates reasonable based on the current Platform Positioning project stage?

619. Was the Platform Positioning project schedule reviewed by all stakeholders and formally accepted?

620. Is current scope of the Platform Positioning project substantially different than that originally defined?

2.30 Communications Management Plan: Platform Positioning

621. How do you manage communications?

622. Why manage stakeholders?

623. Do you then often overlook a key stakeholder or stakeholder group?

624. How is this initiative related to other portfolios, programs, or Platform Positioning projects?

625. What are the interrelationships?

626. Who have you worked with in past, similar initiatives?

627. Are others needed?

628. How will the person responsible for executing the communication item be notified?

629. What is Platform Positioning project communications management?

630. What is the stakeholders level of authority?

631. Is there an important stakeholder who is actively opposed and will not receive messages?

632. Who did you turn to if you had questions?

633. Do you prepare stakeholder engagement plans?

634. Timing: when do the effects of the communication take place?

635. Are stakeholders internal or external?

636. Is the stakeholder role recognized by your organization?

637. Who to learn from?

638. How much time does it take to do it?

639. Are you constantly rushing from meeting to meeting?

2.31 Risk Management Plan: Platform Positioning

640. Market risk -will the new service or product be useful to your organization or marketable to others?

641. What is the cost to the Platform Positioning project if it does occur?

642. What risks are tracked?

643. Is a software Platform Positioning project management tool available?

644. What will drive change?

645. What does a risk management program do?

646. Why do you need to manage Platform Positioning project Risk?

647. Is the customer willing to establish rapid communication links with the developer?

648. Do requirements put excessive performance constraints on the product?

649. How would you suggest monitoring for risk transition indicators?

650. Are there alternative opinions/solutions/ processes you should explore?

651. How much risk protection can you afford?

652. Who/what can assist?

653. Mitigation -how can you avoid the risk?

654. Is the process being followed?

655. Workarounds are determined during which step of risk management?

656. Minimize cost and financial risk?

657. What risks are necessary to achieve success?

658. Internal technical and management reviews?

659. Are enough people available?

2.32 Risk Register: Platform Positioning

660. User involvement: do you have the right users?

661. Are your objectives at risk?

662. What will be done?

663. Who is accountable?

664. Assume the event happens, what is the Most Likely impact?

665. Do you require further engagement?

666. Financial risk -can your organization afford to undertake the Platform Positioning project?

667. When would you develop a risk register?

668. What is a Risk?

669. Manageability – have mitigations to the risk been identified?

670. What evidence do you have to justify the likelihood score of the risk (audit, incident report, claim, complaints, inspection, internal review)?

671. Recovery actions - planned actions taken once a risk has occurred to allow you to move on. What should you do after?

672. Can the likelihood and impact of failing to achieve corresponding recommendations and action plans be assessed?

673. Assume the risk event or situation happens, what would the impact be?

674. What risks might negatively or positively affect achieving the Platform Positioning project objectives?

675. What could prevent you delivering on the strategic program objectives and what is being done to mitigate corresponding issues?

676. Methodology: how will risk management be performed on this Platform Positioning project?

677. Cost/benefit – how much will the proposed mitigations cost and how does this cost compare with the potential cost of the risk event/situation should it occur?

678. Amongst the action plans and recommendations that you have to introduce are there some that could stop or delay the overall program?

679. Who needs to know about this?

2.33 Probability and Impact Assessment: Platform Positioning

680. Anticipated volatility of the requirements?

681. What should be the level of difficulty in handling the technology?

682. How do risks change during the Platform Positioning projects life cycle?

683. Who has experience with this?

684. What significant shift will occur in governmental policies, laws, and regulations pertaining to specific industries?

685. Is the delay in one subPlatform Positioning project going to affect another?

686. Does the customer understand the software process?

687. Will there be an increase in the political conservatism?

688. Have decisions that should be left open because of inadequate information on technology been identified and responsibility assigned for reducing the uncertainty?

689. When and how will the recent breakthroughs in basic research lead to commercial products?

690. What kind of preparation would be required to do this?

691. What things might go wrong?

692. Are trained personnel, including supervisors and Platform Positioning project managers, available to handle such a large Platform Positioning project?

693. How solid is the Platform Positioning projection of competitive reaction?

694. What will be the likely political environment during the life of the Platform Positioning project?

695. What are the risks involved in appointing external agencies to manage the Platform Positioning project?

696. Supply/demand Platform Positioning projections and trends; what are the levels of accuracy?

697. Can you stabilize dynamic risk factors?

698. Can the risk be avoided by choosing a different alternative?

2.34 Probability and Impact Matrix: Platform Positioning

699. Were there any Platform Positioning projects similar to this one in existence?

700. How do you analyze the risks in the different types of Platform Positioning projects?

701. What should be done with non-critical risks?

702. What are the current or emerging trends of culture?

703. How do you define a risk?

704. What will the damage be?

705. What can you do about it?

706. What has the Platform Positioning project manager forgotten to do?

707. Does the Platform Positioning project team have experience with the technology to be implemented?

708. Are there new risks that mitigation strategies might introduce?

709. Mandated delivery date?

710. Do you have a consistent repeatable process that is actually used?

711. What will be the likely incidence of conflict with neighboring Platform Positioning projects?

712. Can the Platform Positioning project proceed without assuming the risk?

713. While preparing your risk responses, you identify additional risks. What should you do?

714. How do risks change during the Platform Positioning projects life cycle?

715. What is your anticipated volatility of the requirements?

716. Have customers been involved fully in the definition of requirements?

717. Are staff committed for the duration of the Platform Positioning project?

2.35 Risk Data Sheet: Platform Positioning

718. Is the data sufficiently specified in terms of the type of failure being analyzed, and its frequency or probability?

719. How reliable is the data source?

720. Type of risk identified?

721. How do you handle product safely?

722. What are the main threats to your existence?

723. Potential for recurrence?

724. If it happens, what are the consequences?

725. Will revised controls lead to tolerable risk levels?

726. Do effective diagnostic tests exist?

727. What was measured?

728. What were the Causes that contributed?

729. What are you trying to achieve (Objectives)?

730. Has the most cost-effective solution been chosen?

731. What are you weak at and therefore need to do

better?

732. What are you here for (Mission)?

733. What will be the consequences if the risk happens?

734. What will be the consequences if it happens?

735. What are your core values?

2.36 Procurement Management Plan: Platform Positioning

736. Platform Positioning project Objectives?

737. How will you coordinate Procurement with aspects of the Platform Positioning project?

738. Is Platform Positioning project status reviewed with the steering and executive teams at appropriate intervals?

739. Are changes in deliverable commitments agreed to by all affected groups & individuals?

740. How will multiple providers be managed?

741. What are things that you need to improve?

742. Why is procurement planning important?

743. Have the key functions and capabilities been defined and assigned to each release or iteration?

744. Has the budget been baselined?

745. Are parking lot items captured?

746. Is there a procurement management plan in place?

747. Have the procedures for identifying budget variances been followed?

748. Is pert / critical path or equivalent methodology being used?

749. Does the Platform Positioning project have a Quality Culture?

750. Are risk oriented checklists used during risk identification?

751. Is there a set of procedures defining the scope, procedures, and deliverables defining quality control?

752. Has the Platform Positioning project manager been identified?

753. Are the schedule estimates reasonable given the Platform Positioning project?

754. Have activity relationships and interdependencies within tasks been adequately identified?

2.37 Source Selection Criteria: Platform Positioning

755. How should comments received in response to a RFP be handled?

756. Comparison of each offers prices to the estimated prices -are there significant differences?

757. What is the basis of an estimate and what assumptions were made?

758. How can solicitation Schedules be improved to yield more effective price competition?

759. How much weight should be placed on past performance information?

760. Who is on the Source Selection Advisory Committee?

761. How organization are proposed quotes/prices?

762. Are they compliant with all technical requirements?

763. Which contract type places the most risk on the seller?

764. What should be the contracting officers strategy?

765. What evidence should be provided regarding proposal evaluations?

766. When is it appropriate to issue a Draft Request for Proposal (DRFP)?

767. Who is entitled to a debriefing?

768. What should communications be used to accomplish?

769. How and when do you enter into Platform Positioning project Procurement Management?

770. Does an evaluation need to include the identification of strengths and weaknesses?

771. When should debriefings be held and how should they be scheduled?

772. What are the guidelines regarding award without considerations?

773. Are resultant proposal revisions allowed?

2.38 Stakeholder Management Plan: Platform Positioning

774. Has the business need been clearly defined?

775. Are all vendor contracts closed out?

776. Are milestone deliverables effectively tracked and compared to Platform Positioning project plan?

777. Is there an on-going process in place to monitor Platform Positioning project risks?

778. Have Platform Positioning project management standards and procedures been identified / established and documented?

779. When would you develop a Platform Positioning project Business Plan?

780. Where are the verification requirements to be documented (eg purchase order, agreement etc)?

781. Is an industry recognized mechanized support tool(s) being used for Platform Positioning project scheduling & tracking?

782. Is a payment system in place with proper reviews and approvals?

783. Is there a Steering Committee in place?

784. If a problem has been detected, what tools can

be used to determine a root cause?

785. Who is responsible for the post implementation review process?

786. Has the schedule been baselined?

787. Are post milestone Platform Positioning project reviews (PMPR) conducted with your organization at least once a year?

2.39 Change Management Plan: Platform Positioning

788. How frequently should you repeat the message?

789. Is there an adequate supply of people for the new roles?

790. Which relationships will change?

791. What risks may occur upfront, during implementation and after implementation?

792. Has the training provider been established?

793. What time commitment will this involve?

794. Do you need new systems?

795. Who might be able to help you the most?

796. What policies and procedures need to be changed?

797. Who will fund the training?

798. How much Platform Positioning project management is needed?

799. Has the priority for this Platform Positioning project been set by the Business Unit Management Team?

800. What is the most positive interpretation it can receive?

801. What is going to be done differently?

802. When to start change management?

803. Is there a support model for this application and are the details available for distribution?

804. What method and medium would you use to announce a message?

805. What processes are in place to manage knowledge about the Platform Positioning project?

806. What does a resilient organization look like?

807. How can you best frame the message so that it addresses the audiences interests?

3.0 Executing Process Group: Platform Positioning

808. How will you know you did it?

809. What does it mean to take a systems view of a Platform Positioning project?

810. What are the typical Platform Positioning project management skills?

811. Do schedule issues conflicts?

812. Specific - is the objective clear in terms of what, how, when, and where the situation will be changed?

813. Are the necessary foundations in place to ensure the sustainability of the results of the programme?

814. Does software appear easy to learn?

815. What are the main types of goods and services being outsourced?

816. What are deliverables of your Platform Positioning project?

817. How does Platform Positioning project management relate to other disciplines?

818. How can you use Microsoft Platform Positioning project and Excel to assist in Platform Positioning project risk management?

819. How do you enter durations, link tasks, and view critical path information?

820. If a risk event occurs, what will you do?

821. How can software assist in Platform Positioning project communications?

822. How does the job market and current state of the economy affect human resource management?

823. What areas were overlooked on this Platform Positioning project?

824. How is Platform Positioning project performance information created and distributed?

825. What type of information goes in the quality assurance plan?

826. What areas does the group agree are the biggest success on the Platform Positioning project?

3.1 Team Member Status Report: Platform Positioning

827. What specific interest groups do you have in place?

828. Does every department have to have a Platform Positioning project Manager on staff?

829. Are the attitudes of staff regarding Platform Positioning project work improving?

830. How does this product, good, or service meet the needs of the Platform Positioning project and your organization as a whole?

831. The problem with Reward & Recognition Programs is that the truly deserving people all too often get left out. How can you make it practical?

832. How will resource planning be done?

833. What is to be done?

834. How can you make it practical?

835. Will the staff do training or is that done by a third party?

836. How much risk is involved?

837. Is there evidence that staff is taking a more professional approach toward management of your

organizations Platform Positioning projects?

838. How it is to be done?

839. Are the products of your organizations Platform Positioning projects meeting customers objectives?

840. Does the product, good, or service already exist within your organization?

841. Do you have an Enterprise Platform Positioning project Management Office (EPMO)?

842. Does your organization have the means (staff, money, contract, etc.) to produce or to acquire the product, good, or service?

843. Why is it to be done?

844. When a teams productivity and success depend on collaboration and the efficient flow of information, what generally fails them?

845. Are your organizations Platform Positioning projects more successful over time?

3.2 Change Request: Platform Positioning

846. What are the basic mechanics of the Change Advisory Board (CAB)?

847. Is it feasible to use requirements attributes as predictors of reliability?

848. What is the purpose of change control?

849. What should be regulated in a change control operating instruction?

850. What are the requirements for urgent changes?

851. For which areas does this operating procedure apply?

852. Will all change requests be unconditionally tracked through this process?

853. Change request coordination ?

854. What is the change request log?

855. How many times must the change be modified or presented to the change control board before it is approved?

856. How are changes graded and who is responsible for the rating?

857. What are the duties of the change control team?

858. How is the change documented (format, content, storage)?

859. How many lines of code must be changed to implement the change?

860. How do you get changes (code) out in a timely manner?

861. How are the measures for carrying out the change established?

862. Are there requirements attributes that are strongly related to the occurrence of defects and failures?

863. Screen shots or attachments included in a Change Request?

864. What is the function of the change control committee?

865. Who is responsible to authorize changes?

3.3 Change Log: Platform Positioning

866. Is the change request open, closed or pending?

867. Who initiated the change request?

868. Will the Platform Positioning project fail if the change request is not executed?

869. Is this a mandatory replacement?

870. Should a more thorough impact analysis be conducted?

871. How does this change affect scope?

872. Is the change backward compatible without limitations?

873. How does this relate to the standards developed for specific business processes?

874. Is the submitted change a new change or a modification of a previously approved change?

875. Does the suggested change request seem to represent a necessary enhancement to the product?

876. How does this change affect the timeline of the schedule?

877. Do the described changes impact on the integrity or security of the system?

878. When was the request submitted?

879. Is the requested change request a result of changes in other Platform Positioning project(s)?

880. Does the suggested change request represent a desired enhancement to the products functionality?

881. Is the change request within Platform Positioning project scope?

882. When was the request approved?

3.4 Decision Log: Platform Positioning

883. Is everything working as expected?

884. How do you define success?

885. Does anything need to be adjusted?

886. It becomes critical to track and periodically revisit both operational effectiveness; Are you noticing all that you need to, and are you interpreting what you see effectively?

887. Adversarial environment. is your opponent open to a non-traditional workflow, or will it likely challenge anything you do?

888. What is the average size of your matters in an applicable measurement?

889. How does the use a Decision Support System influence the strategies/tactics or costs?

890. Is your opponent open to a non-traditional workflow, or will it likely challenge anything you do?

891. What was the rationale for the decision?

892. Decision-making process; how will the team make decisions?

893. What is your overall strategy for quality control / quality assurance procedures?

894. Meeting purpose; why does this team meet?

895. With whom was the decision shared or considered?

896. What alternatives/risks were considered?

897. How do you know when you are achieving it?

898. How does provision of information, both in terms of content and presentation, influence acceptance of alternative strategies?

899. How consolidated and comprehensive a story can you tell by capturing currently available incident data in a central location and through a log of key decisions during an incident?

900. What is the line where eDiscovery ends and document review begins?

901. How does an increasing emphasis on cost containment influence the strategies and tactics used?

902. Who is the decisionmaker?

3.5 Quality Audit: Platform Positioning

903. How does your organization know that its general support services planning and management systems are appropriately effective and constructive?

904. Are all employees made aware of device defects which may occur from the improper performance of specific jobs?

905. How does your organization know that its support services planning and management systems are appropriately effective and constructive?

906. Is your organizational structure established and each positions responsibility defined?

907. Are all records associated with the reconditioning of a device maintained for a minimum of two years after the sale or disposal of the last device within a lot of merchandise?

908. Are measuring and test equipment that have been placed out of service suitably identified and excluded from use in any device reconditioning operation?

909. How does your organization know that its staff entrance standards are appropriately effective and constructive and being implemented consistently?

910. How does your organization know that its

system for managing intellectual property issues is appropriately effective, constructive and fair?

911. How does your organization know that its staff embody the core knowledge, skills and characteristics for which it wishes to be recognized?

912. Are all complaints involving the possible failure of a device, labeling, or packaging to meet any of its specifications reviewed, evaluated, and investigated?

913. How does your organization know that its relationships with other relevant organizations are appropriately effective and constructive?

914. How does your organization ensure that equipment is appropriately maintained and producing valid results?

915. Are salvageable and salvaged medical devices stored in a manner to prevent damage and/or contamination?

916. For each device to be reconditioned, are device specifications, such as appropriate engineering drawings, component specifications and software specifications, maintained?

917. How does your organization know that its system for governing staff behaviour is appropriately effective and constructive?

918. What are you trying to accomplish with this audit?

919. How does your organization know that its

staff placements are appropriately effective and constructive in relation to program-related learning outcomes?

920. Are all areas associated with the storage and reconditioning of devices clean, free of rubbish, adequately ventilated and in good repair?

921. How does your organization know that its advisory services are appropriately effective and constructive?

922. How does your organization know that its Strategic Plan is providing the best guidance for the future of your organization?

3.6 Team Directory: Platform Positioning

923. What needs to be communicated?

924. Is construction on schedule?

925. Where will the product be used and/or delivered or built when appropriate?

926. Have you decided when to celebrate the Platform Positioning projects completion date?

927. Why is the work necessary?

928. What are you going to deliver or accomplish?

929. Process decisions: are all start-up, turn over and close out requirements of the contract satisfied?

930. Contract requirements complied with?

931. Who are the Team Members?

932. Decisions: what could be done better to improve the quality of the constructed product?

933. Timing: when do the effects of communication take place?

934. How do unidentified risks impact the outcome of the Platform Positioning project?

935. Where should the information be distributed?

936. Process decisions: is work progressing on schedule and per contract requirements?

937. Days from the time the issue is identified?

938. Who should receive information (all stakeholders)?

939. When will you produce deliverables?

940. How will the team handle changes?

941. Process decisions: are there any statutory or regulatory issues relevant to the timely execution of work?

3.7 Team Operating Agreement: Platform Positioning

942. What types of accommodations will be formulated and put in place for sustaining the team?

943. Do you send out the agenda and meeting materials in advance?

944. Do you ask participants to close laptops and place mobile devices on silent on the table while the meeting is in progress?

945. What are the safety issues/risks that need to be addressed and/or that the team needs to consider?

946. Do you leverage technology engagement tools group chat, polls, screen sharing, etc.?

947. Do you post any action items, due dates, and responsibilities on the team website?

948. Do you ensure that all participants know how to use the required technology?

949. What is the anticipated procedure (recruitment, solicitation of volunteers, or assignment) for selecting team members?

950. What is culture?

951. How does teaming fit in with overall organizational goals and meet organizational needs?

952. What is group supervision?

953. Why does your organization want to participate in teaming?

954. Must your members collaborate successfully to complete Platform Positioning projects?

955. Have you established procedures that team members can follow to work effectively together, such as a team operating agreement?

956. Are there more than two native languages represented by your team?

957. Methodologies: how will key team processes be implemented, such as training, research, work deliverable production, review and approval processes, knowledge management, and meeting procedures?

958. What are the current caseload numbers in the unit?

959. Do you determine the meeting length and time of day?

960. Did you determine the technology methods that best match the messages to be communicated?

961. Are there more than two functional areas represented by your team?

3.8 Team Performance Assessment: Platform Positioning

962. To what degree are the teams goals and objectives clear, simple, and measurable?

963. How do you recognize and praise members for contributions?

964. Do friends perform better than acquaintances?

965. To what degree does the teams purpose constitute a broader, deeper aspiration than just accomplishing short-term goals?

966. What structural changes have you made or are you preparing to make?

967. Social categorization and intergroup behaviour: Does minimal intergroup discrimination make social identity more positive?

968. When does the medium matter?

969. To what degree do team members understand one anothers roles and skills?

970. How do you keep key people outside the group informed about its accomplishments?

971. To what degree can team members frequently and easily communicate with one another?

972. To what degree can the team measure progress against specific goals?

973. When a reviewer complains about method variance, what is the essence of the complaint?

974. To what degree do members articulate the goals beyond the team membership?

975. To what degree does the teams work approach provide opportunity for members to engage in open interaction?

976. To what degree will the team adopt a concrete, clearly understood, and agreed-upon approach that will result in achievement of the teams goals?

977. To what degree can team members vigorously define the teams purpose in considerations with others who are not part of the functioning team?

978. To what degree are staff involved as partners in the improvement process?

979. To what degree are the relative importance and priority of the goals clear to all team members?

980. To what degree do team members frequently explore the teams purpose and its implications?

981. How much interpersonal friction is there in your team?

3.9 Team Member Performance Assessment: Platform Positioning

982. How is the timing of assessments organized (e.g., pre/post-test, single point during training, multiple reassessment during training)?

983. What resources do you need?

984. How do you know that all team members are learning?

985. Can your organization rate by exception and assume that most employees are performing at an acceptable level?

986. To what extent are systems and applications (e.g., game engine, mobile device platform) utilized?

987. What entity leads the process, selects a potential restructuring option and develops the plan?

988. New skills/knowledge gained this year?

989. Does adaptive training work?

990. What innovations (if any) are developed to realize goals?

991. How effective is training that is delivered through technology-based platforms?

992. How do you determine which data are the most

important to use, analyze, or review?

993. How are evaluation results utilized?

994. How often are assessments to be conducted?

995. What instructional strategies were developed/ incorporated (e.g., direct instruction, indirect instruction, experiential learning, independent study, interactive instruction)?

996. How do you make use of research?

997. Does the rater (supervisor) have to wait for the interim or final performance assessment review to tell an employee that the employees performance is unsatisfactory?

998. To what degree does the team possess adequate membership to achieve its ends?

999. How do you currently use the time that is available?

3.10 Issue Log: Platform Positioning

1000. Who do you turn to if you have questions?

1001. Can an impact cause deviation beyond team, stage or Platform Positioning project tolerances?

1002. Are the stakeholders getting the information they need, are they consulted, are concerns addressed?

1003. Persistence; will users learn a work around or will they be bothered every time?

1004. What would have to change?

1005. Is access to the Issue Log controlled?

1006. Who were proponents/opponents?

1007. How often do you engage with stakeholders?

1008. Who needs to know and how much?

1009. What steps can you take for positive relationships?

1010. Do you often overlook a key stakeholder or stakeholder group?

1011. Who reported the issue?

1012. Is the issue log kept in a safe place?

1013. What is the status of the issue?

1014. What approaches to you feel are the best ones to use?

1015. What date was the issue resolved?

1016. Do you have members of your team responsible for certain stakeholders?

1017. What is the impact on the Business Case?

1018. Why multiple evaluators?

4.0 Monitoring and Controlling Process Group: Platform Positioning

1019. Change, where should you look for problems?

1020. What departments are involved in its daily operation?

1021. How many potential communications channels exist on the Platform Positioning project?

1022. Mitigate. what will you do to minimize the impact should a risk event occur?

1023. How is agile portfolio management done?

1024. What areas were overlooked on this Platform Positioning project?

1025. Where is the Risk in the Platform Positioning project?

1026. What good practices or successful experiences or transferable examples have been identified?

1027. What resources are necessary?

1028. Who are the Platform Positioning project stakeholders?

1029. In what way has the program come up with innovative measures for problem-solving?

1030. What do they need to know about the Platform Positioning project?

1031. Is it what was agreed upon?

1032. Do the products created live up to the necessary quality?

1033. How were collaborations developed, and how are they sustained?

1034. What is the timeline for the Platform Positioning project?

4.1 Project Performance Report: Platform Positioning

1035. What is the PRS?

1036. How is the data used?

1037. What is the degree to which rules govern information exchange between groups?

1038. To what degree does the teams work approach provide opportunity for members to engage in results-based evaluation?

1039. To what degree does the information network communicate information relevant to the task?

1040. To what degree are the demands of the task compatible with and converge with the relationships of the informal organization?

1041. To what degree does the formal organization make use of individual resources and meet individual needs?

1042. How can Platform Positioning project sustainability be maintained?

1043. To what degree will team members, individually and collectively, commit time to help themselves and others learn and develop skills?

1044. To what degree does the teams approach to its

work allow for modification and improvement over time?

1045. To what degree can all members engage in open and interactive considerations?

1046. To what degree do individual skills and abilities match task demands?

1047. To what degree is the information network consistent with the structure of the formal organization?

1048. How will procurement be coordinated with other Platform Positioning project aspects, such as scheduling and performance reporting?

4.2 Variance Analysis: Platform Positioning

1049. What are the actual costs to date?

1050. Does the contractors system provide unit or lot costs when applicable?

1051. What are the direct labor dollars and/or hours?

1052. Are the requirements for all items of overhead established by rational, traceable processes?

1053. What is the budgeted cost for work scheduled?

1054. What costs are avoidable if one or more customers are dropped?

1055. Do the rates and prices remain constant throughout the year?

1056. What is the performance to date and material commitment?

1057. What does an unfavorable overhead volume variance mean?

1058. How do you evaluate the impact of schedule changes, work around, et?

1059. Are records maintained to show how undistributed budgets are controlled?

1060. How are variances affected by multiple material and labor categories?

1061. Are the bases and rates for allocating costs from each indirect pool consistently applied?

1062. What is the incurrence of actual indirect costs in excess of budgets, by element of expense?

1063. Did a new competitor enter the market?

1064. Contract line items and end items?

1065. Are the overhead pools formally and adequately identified?

1066. What is the expected future profitability of each customer?

4.3 Earned Value Status: Platform Positioning

1067. Where is evidence-based earned value in your organization reported?

1068. Where are your problem areas?

1069. How does this compare with other Platform Positioning projects?

1070. If earned value management (EVM) is so good in determining the true status of a Platform Positioning project and Platform Positioning project its completion, why is it that hardly any one uses it in information systems related Platform Positioning projects?

1071. Are you hitting your Platform Positioning projects targets?

1072. Validation is a process of ensuring that the developed system will actually achieve the stakeholders desired outcomes; Are you building the right product? What do you validate?

1073. What is the unit of forecast value?

1074. Verification is a process of ensuring that the developed system satisfies the stakeholders agreements and specifications; Are you building the product right? What do you verify?

1075. Earned value can be used in almost any Platform Positioning project situation and in almost any Platform Positioning project environment. it may be used on large Platform Positioning projects, medium sized Platform Positioning projects, tiny Platform Positioning projects (in cut-down form), complex and simple Platform Positioning projects and in any market sector. some people, of course, know all about earned value, they have used it for years - but perhaps not as effectively as they could have?

1076. When is it going to finish?

1077. How much is it going to cost by the finish?

4.4 Risk Audit: Platform Positioning

1078. Are risk assessments documented?

1079. What are the benefits of a Enterprise wide approach to Risk Management?

1080. Do you have an understanding of insurance claims processes?

1081. Is your organization able to present documentary evidence in support of compliance?

1082. Number of users of the product?

1083. Has risk management been considered when planning an event?

1084. What impact does experience with one client have on decisions made for other clients during the risk-assessment process?

1085. Is the customer willing to participate in reviews?

1086. Assessing risk with analytical procedures: do systemsthinking tools help auditors focus on diagnostic patterns?

1087. How risk averse are you?

1088. Do you record and file all audits?

1089. Who is responsible for what?

1090. Can assurance be expanded beyond the traditional audit without undermining independence?

1091. What are the strategic implications with clients when auditors focus audit resources based on business-level risks?

1092. Who audits the auditor?

1093. When your organization is entering into a major contract, does it seek legal advice?

1094. How do you prioritize risks?

1095. Is the customer technically sophisticated in the product area?

1096. What does your data tell you about your risks?

1097. What are the outcomes you are looking for?

4.5 Contractor Status Report: Platform Positioning

1098. What was the overall budget or estimated cost?

1099. What process manages the contracts?

1100. What are the minimum and optimal bandwidth requirements for the proposed solution?

1101. How is risk transferred?

1102. Who can list a Platform Positioning project as organization experience, your organization or a previous employee of your organization?

1103. What was the final actual cost?

1104. If applicable; describe your standard schedule for new software version releases. Are new software version releases included in the standard maintenance plan?

1105. Are there contractual transfer concerns?

1106. What is the average response time for answering a support call?

1107. How long have you been using the services?

1108. How does the proposed individual meet each requirement?

1109. Describe how often regular updates are made to the proposed solution. Are corresponding regular updates included in the standard maintenance plan?

1110. What was the actual budget or estimated cost for your organizations services?

1111. What was the budget or estimated cost for your organizations services?

4.6 Formal Acceptance: Platform Positioning

1112. Does it do what Platform Positioning project team said it would?

1113. How well did the team follow the methodology?

1114. Have all comments been addressed?

1115. What is the Acceptance Management Process?

1116. What can you do better next time?

1117. Is formal acceptance of the Platform Positioning project product documented and distributed?

1118. Do you perform formal acceptance or burn-in tests?

1119. Was the sponsor/customer satisfied?

1120. Did the Platform Positioning project manager and team act in a professional and ethical manner?

1121. Was business value realized?

1122. Did the Platform Positioning project achieve its MOV?

1123. Was the Platform Positioning project goal achieved?

1124. Does it do what client said it would?

1125. What lessons were learned about your Platform Positioning project management methodology?

1126. Do you buy-in installation services?

1127. What function(s) does it fill or meet?

1128. What features, practices, and processes proved to be strengths or weaknesses?

1129. Who supplies data?

1130. Do you buy pre-configured systems or build your own configuration?

1131. Was the Platform Positioning project work done on time, within budget, and according to specification?

5.0 Closing Process Group: Platform Positioning

1132. How critical is the Platform Positioning project success to the success of your organization?

1133. Was the user/client satisfied with the end product?

1134. Is this a follow-on to a previous Platform Positioning project?

1135. What were things that you did very well and want to do the same again on the next Platform Positioning project?

1136. How well did you do?

1137. What was learned?

1138. Did the delivered product meet the specified requirements and goals of the Platform Positioning project?

1139. What will you do to minimize the impact should a risk event occur?

1140. What areas were overlooked on this Platform Positioning project?

1141. What were things that you did well, and could improve, and how?

1142. What areas does the group agree are the biggest success on the Platform Positioning project?

1143. Does the close educate others to improve performance?

1144. Were sponsors and decision makers available when needed outside regularly scheduled meetings?

1145. What communication items need improvement?

1146. How dependent is the Platform Positioning project on other Platform Positioning projects or work efforts?

1147. Are there funding or time constraints?

5.1 Procurement Audit: Platform Positioning

1148. Does an appropriately qualified official check the quality of performance against the contract terms?

1149. Does the department have a procurement strategy and is it implemented?

1150. Are existing suppliers that have a special right to be consulted being contacted?

1151. Are procurement policies and practices in line with (international) good practice standards?

1152. Are the purchase order forms designed for efficient and simple completion?

1153. Are there complementary rules to be used and are they applied?

1154. Are there established procedures for dealing with and documenting non-performance and return of goods?

1155. Is there a record maintained of the procedures followed in the opening of tenders together with the reasons for the acceptance or rejection of tenders received?

1156. Is there a practice that prohibits signing blank purchase orders?

1157. Are vendor price lists regularly updated?

1158. Did the additional works introduce minor or non-substantial changes to performance, as described in the contract documents?

1159. When you set social or environmental conditions for the performance of the contract, were corresponding compatible with the law and was adequate information given to the candidates?

1160. Is there a form specified for bids?

1161. Are procurement processes well organized and documented?

1162. Does your organization make sources of information beyond the tender documents equally available for all the candidates?

1163. Are all claims certified by the officer giving rise to the claim (usually the purchasing agent)?

1164. Are advantages and disadvantages of in-house production, outsourcing and Public Private Partnerships considered?

1165. Does the strategy include a policy for identifying and training suitable procurement staff?

1166. Who are the key suppliers?

1167. Is it calculated whether aggregated procurement can be more cost-efficient?

5.2 Contract Close-Out: Platform Positioning

1168. Change in knowledge?

1169. Was the contract sufficiently clear so as not to result in numerous disputes and misunderstandings?

1170. Parties: Authorized?

1171. Change in attitude or behavior?

1172. Have all contracts been closed?

1173. Was the contract complete without requiring numerous changes and revisions?

1174. Have all contract records been included in the Platform Positioning project archives?

1175. Are the signers the authorized officials?

1176. Have all contracts been completed?

1177. Change in circumstances?

1178. Have all acceptance criteria been met prior to final payment to contractors?

1179. What is capture management?

1180. What happens to the recipient of services?

1181. Was the contract type appropriate?

1182. How does it work?

1183. Why Outsource?

1184. How is the contracting office notified of the automatic contract close-out?

1185. How/when used ?

1186. Parties: who is involved?

1187. Has each contract been audited to verify acceptance and delivery?

5.3 Project or Phase Close-Out: Platform Positioning

1188. Did the delivered product meet the specified requirements and goals of the Platform Positioning project?

1189. What can you do better next time, and what specific actions can you take to improve?

1190. Who controlled key decisions that were made?

1191. What information did each stakeholder need to contribute to the Platform Positioning projects success?

1192. Were messages directly related to the release strategy or phases of the Platform Positioning project?

1193. Who exerted influence that has positively affected or negatively impacted the Platform Positioning project?

1194. How often did each stakeholder need an update?

1195. Was the schedule met?

1196. Is the lesson based on actual Platform Positioning project experience rather than on independent research?

1197. Were risks identified and mitigated?

1198. How much influence did the stakeholder have over others?

1199. Planned completion date?

1200. When and how were information needs best met?

1201. What were the actual outcomes?

1202. Were cost budgets met?

1203. Does the lesson educate others to improve performance?

1204. Complete yes or no?

1205. Who is responsible for award close-out?

1206. What could be done to improve the process?

5.4 Lessons Learned: Platform Positioning

1207. Who is responsible for each action?

1208. Were the right people available when required?

1209. Do you have any real problems?

1210. What regulatory constraints impact the case?

1211. How effective was the documentation that you received with the Platform Positioning project product/service?

1212. How much of your time was spent on other than this Platform Positioning project?

1213. Would you spend your own money to fix this issue?

1214. Were the aims and objectives achieved?

1215. Did the Platform Positioning project management methodology work?

1216. What regulatory regime controlled how your organization head and program manager directed your organization and Platform Positioning project?

1217. Will the information remain current?

1218. What is the frequency of personal

communications?

1219. Was sufficient time allocated to review Platform Positioning project deliverables?

1220. What are the skills directly related to the task?

1221. How useful was the content of the training you received in preparation for the use of the product/service?

1222. How many government and contractor personnel are authorized for the Platform Positioning project?

1223. What were the key issues?

1224. What is the desired end-state?

1225. Overall, how effective were the efforts to prepare you and your organization for the impact of the product/service of the Platform Positioning project?

1226. How does the budget cycle affect the case?

Index

CPSIA information can be obtained
at www.ICGtesting.com
Printed in the USA
BVHW082019110819
555624BV00016BA/1865/P